Journ

MW00938782

The New Millennium NoteBooks

Volume Eight

COMMUNICATION THROUGH CHANNELING
Journeys in the Present

Norma Hickox

Communication through Channeling
A Chrysalis Publication

ISBN-13:978-1519303295

Published by Chrysalis Publications
email: www.nhickox@gmail.com
web page: www.chrysalispub.com

Photography and Drawings by Neil Hickox
Cover photograph – Power Lines in San Fernando Valley,
CA

Other books by Norma Hickox:
Truths of Man's Divine Heritage Vol. I
Truths of Man's Divine Heritage Vol. II
Cataclysms?? A NEW Look at Earth Changes
The New Millennium NoteBooks:
Windows on the Past
    Vol 1 - The TimeLine of Eternity
    Vol. 2 - The Fantastic Human Being
    Vol. 3 - The Awesome Realm of the Soul
    Vol. 4 - The Exciting New Creation
Journeys in the Present
    Vol. 5 - The Compelling Spiritual Path
    Vol. 6 - The Enlightenment of Self-Knowledge
    Vol. 7 – An Informative Book of Health

PREFACE

The New Millennium NoteBooks, based on The Chrysalis Teachings, will benefit those seeking to become better people by allowing them to ponder the fact that they are not alone in this universe; that there is structure to their path and definite goals ahead to continually strive for.

I believe that these teachings will allow people to finally understand their dual nature; that without allowing the growth of the soul to take place they are not much higher on the evolutionary pole than the animals. Someday the animals will evolve to the same stage as a human who is not expressing the soul. When people begin to understand this, they will begin to look at life differently and will be more willing to stay on the spiritual path of progress

The New Millennium NoteBooks are roadmaps for growth – physically, emotionally, mentally and spiritually, and serve to educate and explain much that remains a mystery. I believe that if people could get a big picture of where they came from and how they developed, it would serve them well in their interactions with each other and help promote peace in the world.

These notebooks cover a wide range of topics encompassing all spiritual disciplines. They are divided into three sections, "Windows on the Past," "Journeys in the Present" and "Pathways to the Future."

FROM THE AUTHOR

I am a professional musician. I play and teach six instruments and compose music. I have been an organist and choir director for many different spiritual denominations and have also taught vocal music in private elementary and pre-schools. In the past I played in the pit orchestra for a musical theater group and also in a dance band, eventually having my own dance band. I have played numerous solo appearances, some on TV and played a Christmas Eve church service for former President Ford and his family in Vail, Colorado. Along with music, my career has also included involvement with the arts of painting, writing, dance and theater that led to my writing two musical plays with original music.

I live with my son Neil and his family, wife Claudia, daughter Fiorella and son Leland in Simi Valley, California. Neil did the artwork for all of the New Millennium Notebooks. He is a computer scientist and amateur photographer. Without his help not only for the artwork, but also in keeping my computer operating properly, these books probably would not have come into being.

I've been blessed with the privilege or gift of "knowing" many spiritual truths. It seems that some part of my makeup has the ability to "know" and "see" into different time periods of the past. I call this higher aspect of my soul the "Timetraveler." Actually, being a musician, it was the vibrations of music that I've been exposed to since the age of four that enables me to have this insight. The TimeTraveler is the transformer of the vibrations and the

iv

interpreter of higher plane information on which I rely to understand the thought picture I access.

The Time Traveler

The TimeTraveler rides on his magic carpet of time powered by the vibration of the colors of the rainbow which match the vibrations of the musical scale of C. The TimeTraveler himself vibrates at the tone of "middle C." He has the ability to travel instantly to any time period of the universe. A small picture of him will appear at the beginning of the material given by the TimeTraveler for each chapter.

I hope you will allow yourself to imagine that perhaps I have been given incredible insight into some of the mysteries of the universe. Please allow your mind to expand and wonder "what if" it all took place as shown to me.

These teachings will clearly show that
Birth (Creation) and Development (Evolution)
go hand in hand. You cannot have one without the
other.

"Finding God" – Poem by Norma

Who needs a God sitting on a throne,
With capes of fur and crown of gold?
Not I, cried an enlightened few,
To whom the truth had been told.

He is not up in the sky where you look,
And the more you search in vain,
The farther away He will seem to be,
And the deeper your feeling of pain.

Bring Him out of the vastness of space;
Bring him back down to earth.
This is where you'll find God, my friend,
He's been with you since birth.

For God is your own soul, dear one,
Knowing this, all will fall in place.
For if you put Him on a throne, my friend,
You'll be worshiping your very own face.

Is this what you want; one to lean on?
Won't you listen for what rings true?
Search yourself and find Him inside,
Not on a cloud, but deep within you.

TABLE OF CONTENTS

INTRODUCTION 1

Chapter 1: CHANNELING IS VOICE OF SPIRIT 3

Chapter 2: OLD AND NEW WAYS OF CHANNELING .. 21

Chapter 3: THE FOUNTAIN OF KNOWLEDGE 37

Chapter 4: FORMING THE RINGS OF ENERGY 53

Chapter 5: RINGS LIKE CLIMBING STAIRWAY 71

Chapter 6: MY PERSONAL EXPERIENCES 87

Chapter 7: A REVIEW 111

Chapter 8: STEP UP IN MENTAL PROCESSES 129

Chapter 9: CONTACT WITH MUSICAL UNIVERSE . 155

Chapter 10: THE SYNTHESIZED CHANNEL 173

Chapter 11: THE SPACESHIP PHENOMENA 207

Chapter 12: UFOS OUTSIDE OUR SOLAR SYSTEM ... 219

INTRODUCTION

Under the banner of "Journeys in the Present," this eighth volume is "Communication through Channeling." The part of the Creator's mind in residence in our galaxy eventually realized there was much more He could experience if He could become small enough to inhabit some of the animal forms that were developing according to evolution (which in reality is a scientific reaction to circumstances) on some of the planets He had made. He chose to experience more of life on one particular planet in one particular solar system, planet earth, because it had many different animal forms evolving on it. This piece of the Creator's mind was a large, ungainly, awkward field of energy to try to explore this fascinating new planet with, so the decision was made to split His energy apart into small pieces and let each piece, or spark of His energy, explore on its own. This was done, and the sparks of the Creator (spirits) were able to enter the animal forms and learn to express through them.

When the Sparks entered the physical bodies it was never intended that they should loose contact with the main body of the Creator God that stayed in the higher realms. The plan was to always have open lines of communication. Channeling is part of the plan as it allows this communication to take place – from the Creator's mind to the mind of humans, to the Conglomerate Mind of the Micro Men (the Kingdom of God is Within) and back again to the Creator's mind. Channeling is the mechanism by which the cycle of evolution is accomplished on the earth plane. Therefore, channeling is a natural, normal stage of evolution for humanity, whose time has come.

Chapter 1

CHANNELING IS THE VOICE OF SPIRIT

"Look at this picture you took of wind turbines. It makes a pretty picture doesn't it?" I asked Neil.

We were going through the pictures on my computer to clean them up and consolidate them into files.

"Yeah, I thought it made a neat picture," Neil replied.

Wind Turbines

"You know, these wind turbines stretching off into the distance as far as the eye can see are exactly what our lines of communication with the spiritual world do. They stretch back as far as we are able to reach, even to the beginning of time." I said.

"That's an interesting analogy," Neil answered. "I bet you're going to elaborate on it by contacting the TimeTraveler," he continued, smiling.

"You got it," I replied. "I know that he had an awful lot to say about communication between dimensions. We call it channeling but actually the word channeling has gotten kind of a bad name, lately," I said.

"I guess it has. Maybe the TimeTraveler can explain it so that people can understand it and know that it's not the work of evil forces," Neil answered.

"Let's contact him now and see what he has to say," I replied.

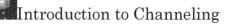Introduction to Channeling

The New Millennium Teachings can explain many things that are not clear to us even with all the other teachings we have at our disposal, including the Bible. The Bible is truly the Word of our Creator sent down through His communicators. The New Millennium Teachings are also the Word of our Creator sent down through this particular communicator. The newer teachings are much clearer to understand as they do not have the misinterpretation of centuries-old communications and have not been through the translation from other languages. Also, they are being communicated from the unseen or unmanifested state by more highly evolved spiritual beings. It is my hope that these teachings will help many on their spiritual path and enable them to tie these teachings in with Biblical teachings.

4

Creation and Evolution Go Hand In Hand

The New Millennium Teachings are based on the fact that Creation and Evolution go hand in hand – that one cannot exist  without the other. The mind of the Creator was given birth at original creation at the time of the "Big Bang." The Creator was able to induce evolution to a point where the planets, suns and stars were also given birth. As each large piece of the Creator's mind broke away from the original it took up residence and expressed through the planets, suns and stars.

The piece of the Creator's mind that chose to experience more of life on planet earth was a large, ungainly, awkward field of energy to try to explore this fascinating new planet with. The decision was made to split His energy apart into small pieces and let each piece, or spark of His energy, explore on its own. In the beginning these sparks were whole sparks, male and female together until the sparks were split in half at the time of Atlantis, (the story of Adam and Eve). You see, the real meaning of the story of Adam and Eve had nothing whatsoever to do with the physical body. The physical forms had evolved into either male or female and the sparks (spirits) trying to enter them were both male and female combined. This did not work and the sparks were split into male and female, positive and negative energy with only one half being allowed to incarnate into a physical form at any one time. The other half had to stay on the inner planes to guide the incarnation from there. The purpose, the plan, of earth

5

plane existence was for each of these male and female halves, to learn, grow and experience and to synthesize their animal nature with their divine nature, so they could become a complete composite of both the Biological Kingdom and the Divine Kingdom, and a new kingdom, the Human Kingdom, was brought into existence. This was also the time when the restructuring of the chakras was done by closing some chakras and enhancing others and the new brain was brought into existence (the Biblical fall of man). (For a fuller explanation of this see Volume Three of the New Millennium NoteBooks, "The Fantastic Human Being.")

The Sparks were Not Meant to Lose Contact with the Creator

Channeling is the voice of the spirit within each human being; it is the voice of your God Within, if you will. It is within everyone, let there be no mistake about it. As to whether it is reached or not depends on many things.

Anyone can do it. In fact, many already do channeling and have just accepted it as a part of them and never questioned where this inner voice came from. They are the ones who have already bonded with this inner part, or become synthesized (joined lower and higher selves) in other lifetimes. You will find them at a higher level of intelligence. This is what it's all about after all – achieving the higher mind, which simply will be seen as higher intelligence.

Channeling Different for All

Channeling takes many different forms with many different people. It won't always be as words being heard in your head or thought pictures. It could come just as thoughts. If this is the way a channel is developing it will most likely be a vocal channel as opposed to a writing channel. This person will speak the thoughts. This is his form of channeling, instead of writing the thoughts. It is every bit as valid a channel as the written channel.

There are others who bring this channel through the arts, who channel inspiration from the higher realms into their paintings, into their music, and most definitely into theatrical performances. The making of a great actor is his ability to channel the thought processes of the character he is developing (this is a slightly different meaning of the term channeling). He actually gives birth to this character inside his mind and channels that through. This would be a form of "brain channeling." That kind of acting is in a category by itself. This does not apply to art and music. Art and music are simply a different language for expressing the thought patterns, the thought pictures that come through from the higher realms. One person will bring these through in writing, another in speaking, others in painting, music, dance, or perhaps skating. Any of these arts – the movement, and the patterns, the colors and the harmonies – are all being channeled. When a writer writes the channeling, these are all there in the writing. As a matter of fact, if a channel were to write in different colors when at the computer, it would make the interpretation of the material easier.

Understanding of Channeling is Progressing

With the breakthrough into the understanding of channeling – which is part of our divine heritage – much forward progress has been made. The ability to do channeling was looked upon as witchcraft for many centuries, even to the point of "burning at the stake" those who did this. Do you realize the significant progress that has been achieved in the last few years? Can you imagine the reaction to a show such as Shirley MacLaine's "Out on a Limb" even 15 or 20 years ago?

Thousands of years ago, only those with a highly evolved background could do this channeling. Thus they were, and rightly should have been, revered as teachers and prophets. But the level they reached with their channeling was not nearly as high a source as most today are capable of reaching. (When Master Jesus said, "What I do, you can do also," could it have been channeling he was speaking of?) There were not as many highly evolved souls in the other dimensions, at that time, to respond with intelligence. Therefore, some who could contact other dimensions did so with a lower level of evolved souls. As progress is made on the earth plane, so also in the "voice within" able to make contact with more intelligent thoughts and ideas in the other dimensions.

We are in the early phase of this stage of evolution and many are able to open the channel in this lifetime. Some have opened it in previous lifetimes and many will open it in the following lifetime. Most children being born today will have the channel readily able to open with proper education. Herein lies the only control factor of this stage of evolution – education as to the proper use of the ability to channel. This is the ability to communicate with your

8

inner being, the unseen parts of you that make up the total you.

The Trinity

The Kingdom of God is within and can be reached by channeling the trinity. The trinity that the churches have talked about for so long is made up of the large, all-encompassing mind of the Creator, (Father); the fragmented mind of humans, (Son); and the conglomerate mind of all we have ever been (the Micro Men) that is inside our mind (Holy Ghost). To explain further, the trinity consists of:

1. Macro Universe Channeling (Father) - One part is the divine mind, the Creator God. The Macro Universe, the mind of the Creator, can only see the overview, is concerned with the total self and will evolve by expressing through the Human Universe. The first stage of channeling (communication), as far as the Creator goes, was simply the blending of the crumbling rocks of the Geological Kingdom with each other and with water to produce a soil in which many different forms of the Botanical Kingdom could evolve. The presence of channeling in the Botanical Kingdom is documented by the many varieties of animals that evolved due to the mating of decomposing plants with water. The channeling in the Biological Kingdom is between each species of animals and also with humans. Those of one species will have a communion with each other that is not possible between different species, but there is still a sense of communication between all animals and all humans. They also feel a union with the

Botanical Kingdom, which responds favorably to the Geological Kingdom.

2. Human Universe Channeling (Son) – This is the entities own mind, which is his animal-based brain, infiltrated by thoughts from the divine spark. The Human Universe must be self-centered, as far as its application of the teachings, until it grows to the point of fourth dimensional consciousness. Humans can only see the personal view and are concerned with the personal self. There is a thread of communication between all kingdoms and the human can and does tap into this line of communication almost from the beginning of life. In the womb, he is operating on the theory of communication that was present in the Geological Kingdom. The process of birth itself represents the instinct present in the Botanical Kingdom and the sucking at the breast represents the communication available in the Biological Kingdom, which is also instinct. In other words, the functions of the human body are a combination of the three lower kingdoms. Present day physicians should study this statement in relation to the human digestive system.

3. Micro Universe Channeling (Holy Ghost) - The conglomerate mind is another part of the trinity. This consists of the teachers and guides, entities who have already crossed over and are further ahead on the path than we are, who have reached back to help. They are living, human beings in the unmanifested state. You are a living, human being in the manifested state. The Micro Universe, the conglomerate mind, is not self-centered. It is working on drawing the Creator's kingdoms

10

together in its application of the concepts. It must, of necessity, try to achieve oneness through the kingdoms. It realizes this more fully for having been through all the developmental stages. The conglomerate mind (the Micro Men) can see it all and are not the least concerned with self. The process leading up to the Conglomerate or Micro stage of evolution is long and complicated. The beginning of this stage is the mission that our Master Teacher Jesus came to the earth plane to accomplish – the Kingdom of God is within. Humans need to learn about their divine heritage, which is the creative channel, and about the ultimate goal of using this channel, which is reaching the trinity, (the Kingdom of God is within). Reaching the trinity is having the ability to channel from three areas simultaneously, the mind of the Creator (Father), our own past incarnations (Son), and the Micro Mind, the teachers and guides (Holy Ghost). This then is our God Within.

Instinct Refined to Intuition will open the Channel

As the human progresses he becomes more aware of a feeling of bonding with the different kingdoms at different stages of his growth. At the present time there is no precise order that this awareness progresses through, but it is all leading to the same point – that of instinct becoming refined to intuition. In the future, early schooling will focus on the ability to transmute instinct to intuition. The way to sharpen up the intuition is by interacting with other people and also with the animal and plant kingdoms. Intuition would be an opening of feeling as to what is going on within a plant, sensing, when looking at a plant, what shape or what condition it's in. Is it happy? Does it look sad? Is it undernourished? Is it not loved? Then moving on to the animal, even greater communication is possible. Intuition is a feeling of knowing what a certain animal is all about – how they will react to each situation, depending on their state of physical health at the time. Animals will have the ability to help teach children in the future, as intuition will be learned and practiced with animals first. After a sensing of animals, the human will begin to apply this ability to his fellow humans. This is the beginning of becoming intuitive, which is a forerunner of more in-depth channeling. All this is to sharpen your intuition, not your instinct. Your instinct is a natural, inborn quality that you have; you don't have to sharpen it. It was a gift and it's this instinct that you're transmuting into intuition. Working with plants, animals, and humans, not necessarily in that order, but with all three, will help with the breakthrough into transmuting this intuition into actual channeling.

Intuition is Forerunner to Channeling

When one gets a subtle feeling, or some other subtle communication, this is intuition and is a forerunner of channeling. The intuition needs to be worked on and developed and will eventually turn into actual channeling. You can't say that intuition is a form of channeling but rather that it is a forerunner of the actual process of channeling. Intuition has grown out of instinct of the animal-based brain and is a sign of the beginning influence of the soul on the incarnation.

If you are beginning to get these subtle feelings or some other type of communication, but don't actually hear any words mentally, or get any thought pictures, you have not moved past the stage of intuition. Rather than trying to force open the channel, you need to continue trying to sharpen up the intuition. This will automatically turn into channeling if it is accompanied by study on transmutation of attitudes by meditation processes and a true spiritual desire to be closer to your Creator. It should not be a desire to be able to channel like others who are doing it to gain fame or money and it also shouldn't be just because of all the excitement of doing it. All that will do would be to hold back the process. It must be a true, sincere, deep strong desire within you to be in touch with your Creator.

Arts Help with Heightened Sense of Sight and Hearing

The process begins to follow a definite path at this time, in relationship to the use of the intuition. More use of the intuition will cause other factors of channeling to begin to come into place. A sharpened sense of sight and hearing are two factors. This is one of the areas where the arts have a bearing on channeling. They cause an increased or heightened sense of both of these functions.

When the channel to the inner kingdom, the Micro Universe, is opened slowly through the creative arts, it is a much deeper and more dependable channel than an opening that is forced by quick methods. The person will be much better prepared to handle the energy when it begins to come through if there is a slow opening. The vast amount of people today with mental aberrations will not be present in future generations if the opening of the channel through the creative arts is begun at birth, or shortly thereafter. There is a well-defined path that will open the channel and needs to be begun as a child and carried through all education.

Balance Point for Humanity

The balance point for humanity is to be able to cross dimensions in thinking, speaking and acting in a second's time. The ability to change back and forth as the occasion demands is a point that very few reach. One needs to be as a compass needle that turns and moves with the exoteric stimuli that the form is being bombarded with. This could perhaps be comparable to a sensor on a thermostat that triggers a heating element on and off. This is difficult for those to see who cannot get a grasp on the overall views of humanity. When one is so enmeshed in his personal reality, his personality, he cannot sense himself as a cork bobbing on the water of a lake and needing to be guided to stay on course, or a ship that needs to be kept on course. There are many analogies of what I'm trying to put across. Any one of them will do. The point is, you have this powerhouse to draw from as the occasion calls for, but the "heating element" cannot work if the sensing device controlling the thermostat is not operating. This sensing device in humans is the intuition.

The intuition is a conglomerate of many things. It consists of past experiences, not only of the present life, but from all incarnations. It consists of vibratory rate – the faster the vibration the more keen the intuition. It also consists of diet, which forms fat cells in the brain which hinder intuition from working. Exercise discipline in all areas of life.

Intuition also is a combination of emotional control, perception and interest in others. The list could go on and on. As given, it is a conglomerate that is advising your God Within, that tiny, tiny voice of right and wrong. When you have a "gut" feeling about something, it is probably your intuition. Once this intuition is recognized and proven accurate by a person and thereafter is heeded in his daily life, this person has the necessary sensing device then to trigger the thermostat that starts the guidance correction system into its duties. This is in helping an individual know how to respond to certain situations. The whole process will be slow at first, but with use will become a smooth working process that kicks in and out as needed with help from whatever level of the mind is needed.

If one needs to be able to figure a complicated formula out for a math or science problem, the sensing device triggers the animal brain to call on help from the higher mind at probably level seven. If one is listening to a symphony orchestra needing to write a critical review for instance, the level of six will be called into play. If one is weary and distraught over a situation and feeling very low, the triggering action would automatically take him to level ten, perhaps only momentarily, but enough to give him a glimmer of hope for the future. This would be the ideal way for humans to operate, but it is very difficult to pull it all together.

Any aids that affect the exoteric life for the better will make smoother sailing just by easing the difficult situations one finds oneself in. This is fine, but will not help the esoteric handling of problems. Quite often exoteric aids and exercises will hinder the esoteric growth pattern. This is why it is necessary to try to balance the outer help so it does not overstep the boundaries and take away lessons the soul needs to learn. This happens many times when one goes to a psychic for a "reading." The psychic gives information that the person should be searching himself for by meditation, regressions, dream analysis and studying his Astro-Numero chart. All this would have caused his mind to stretch and grow and start a tiny crack in his seed core. Instead, the knowledge is slapped at him from an exoteric angle (the psychic) and he gains nothing in the way of self-growth. Does this help explain why psychic readings should stop? Humanity will never get their sensing devices working to trigger the response mechanism as long as this practice is continued. This is very important and yes, one must "swim against the tide" to take this stand, but it is a big stumbling block that is being put in the path of many. It is a crutch; it does a person no good as far as his growth and evolvement. Sure it's fun; it's fascinating, but shouldn't people have some more serious things to spend their money on? They can speculate on "past lives" and "present day guides" etc. by having a once a year fun party to this effect, but for heaven's sake do not use this stuff seriously. What good can be gained? Whatever a person is told by a psychic can be found out by the person himself with a little hard work. It is just laziness to go to another.

The results of those who are constantly going to readers do not help. The person usually regresses in that lifetime. If they let their own guides help them, they would re-experience some events that would make an impression on them. Being told something from someone else does not put a dent in the mind of the person whatsoever. The goal of the New Millennium is to eliminate these "psychic readers" and have in their place "counselors" who use a number of methods to open a person's own seed core. The psychics doing readings have stopped their own climb thinking they have reached the ultimate way to serve humanity. This is as wrong in one direction as the churches are in the other direction. The middle path is balance and it is very difficult to find and keep this balance to stay on the middle path as a well-balanced human being on his upward climb to becoming a divine being.

Alpha and Beta Waves

There is a distinct difference in channels because channeling is based on a mathematical progression of absolute perfection. When the channel first opens it must work its way up through the manifested ways of channeling to the unmanifested ways. The first way involves psychic phenomena or mind to mind phenomena, not only human to human, but also human to animal (Biological Kingdom), human to plant, (Botanical Kingdom) and human to mineral (Geological Kingdom). The second way is mind to mind phenomena, human to Prismatic Kingdom, human to Atmospheric Kingdom and human to Astronomical Kingdom.

The channels that use beta waves are the lower kingdom channels. These waves are radiations of the animal-based brain and radiate upward from the lower kingdoms.

Those who use alpha waves are the higher kingdom channels. These waves are radiations of the Divine Mind and radiate downward from the higher kingdoms. Both manifest in the human being. A channel will work from the one state into the next if they continue growing and evolving and raising their consciousness.

The channel begins with mere instinctive actions until awakened by the kingdom ahead of it as to its purpose and ultimate goal. This instinct is responsible for the

17

crumbling of the rocks forming soil that allows the growth and progress of the Botanical Kingdom. The Botanical Kingdom knows instinctively that it will form lower animal forms when it disintegrates, leading to and obliging the Biological Kingdom. The animal part of the Biological Kingdom instinctively knows that it is to help the human part of the Biological Kingdom as workers. They will provide food in many different ways from the honey bee to the horses used for plowing or manure used for fertilizer.

The human part of the Biological Kingdom has the ability to draw on all this instinct and turn it into intuition and be able to "tune in" to all these kingdoms plus their fellow human beings. The human then takes this intuition and hones it to a degree by tuning up his vibrations musically and allowing transcendence or blending of beta and alpha waves to take place. This is the period of psychic phenomena that all go through, must go through, to be able then to draw in the higher energy, that of using the alpha waves. These waves then must be constantly and continuously honed and refined to draw ever higher kingdoms down to them. These higher kingdoms help by sending these waves down as far as they are capable. Channeling the higher energies is a two way process as the higher energies can only be sent down so far with any force. Then the human must strive to reach up to them. The two different energies can be thought of as broad band radio waves and narrow band, involuted radio waves.

Humans are Transformers between Physical Matter and Ethereal Matter

Channeling is an absolutely normal function for human beings. Humans are the link between two different manifestations of the Creator's energy. There are three dimensions lower than the human and three higher. The first seven planets are used for these manifestations of energy. The merging of the lower and higher dimensions takes place in the middle kingdom, the Biological, on the middle planet of the seven, earth.

As the link between the lower and higher dimensions, channeling is of both spiritual and physical importance. It is the line of relationship running through all the kingdoms tying them together and is of a twofold nature. One aspect of it is ESP and intuition which is the natural link-up between kingdoms. The other aspect is the channeling that feeds into the human being from the higher dimensions. The total process is a function of the human form due to its having evolved through all kingdoms on its evolutionary journey, starting with the original Elemental Kingdom and working through the Geological, Botanical and Biological Kingdom.

The higher kingdoms are also a function of the growth and evolution of the human, and eventually the return to the Elemental Kingdom will complete the divine circle and end yet another cycle. The human is the physical manifestation of all aspects of the Creator. It is the only kingdom able to encompass and function through all kingdoms simultaneously. It is a very rare and beautiful kingdom and is of spiritual importance to all universes due to its uniqueness; a marvelous handiwork of the Creator and a scientific research project of His that is still being perfected.

Chapter 2

OLD AND NEW WAYS OF CHANNELING

"Neil, look at this picture of your Aunt Lois that you took with your cell phone. I think it's amazing the things you can do with a cell phone now-a-days," I said.

Neil's Aunt Lois at his wedding taken with his cell phone

"They really can do wonderful things, can't they?" Neil asked.

"I know you don't remember the old-fashioned wall phones where you had to crank the hand crank and an operator came on and asked who you wanted to call. I never had to use one. They're older than my experience with phones," I said.

"No," Neil answered. "I've seen pictures of them and saw them being used on TV shows, but don't think I ever saw one much less ever used one.

"I'll never forget the first time I used a phone. It was a rotary dial phone. Believe it or not it was after your Dad and I were married. I never used one as a child or growing up as a teenager. I never drove a car either until after I was married. But when I used the phone for the first time to call long distance, the operator came on and asked me the number I wanted and it scared me so bad I hung up on her," I continued.

"That seems almost unbelievable in this day and age," Neil responded.

"I know. Communication has progressed so much on the earth plane and actually it has been progressing on the inner planes also in the way that channeling is supposed to take place. Let's check in with the TimeTraveler and find out the difference between channeling now and channeling in the old days," I said

"Okay by me," Neil answered. "I think that will be quite interesting."

Old Way of Channeling

Trance channeling is the "old world" method of channeling. The "new age" method of channeling is conscious channeling. In the old method, the person doing the channeling, the medium, stepped out of the body and let the one coming through use the body. This was mostly

done by entities on the astral plane because they have forms as large as those of us on the earth plane.

Trance channeling is not to go into the new millennium. This is not the correct way to handle channeling. Those who go into a trance are not doing anything different than the mediums with their crystal balls did in the circus many decades ago. This is not what is wanted. Those people teaching trance channeling are doing a disservice to others. They need to understand this so they themselves will grow past what it is they are doing and not encourage others to do it this way. There will be much karma involved for one teaching others "old world" methods.

New Way of Channeling

When channeling is done on the advanced planes, it is through correct esoteric means of using the Micro Universe. This means the entity coming through is no bigger in size on the earth plane than a pin point. The one doing the channeling on the earth plane, (the medium) does not need to vacate the body to allow one this size to come through. They merely "stand behind" the one doing the channeling, if you will. They are still in the body and the switch can be made back and forth from one to the other. Eventually the blending is completed by the higher entity intertwining with the cells of the body and "taking up permanent residence there." This is when total synthesization has been achieved and the medium is in contact with the God Within. The medium will then be talking to the cells of his or her own body. This is the goal. Each one on the earth plane will have their God Within in residence in the body and be operating through divine guidance at all times.

As it is presently, there are many people at all different stages of growth on this progressive path of channeling. They all need to be encouraged to continue moving. As a matter of fact, it has been suggested that channels only give readings for a certain period of time because it holds back their own growth. They should move on and pass the task of giving readings to those just beginning to channel. This will help the beginning channel's growth until he reaches a point where he should move on also. The beginning channels can give more accurate, daily information in the readings than can advanced channels; they can give more information applicable to daily lives. The advanced channels are then free to give teachings applicable for the spiritual lives of humanity.

The true way to channel your divine heritage is to bring it through you as you – as who you are in this lifetime. The giving of names (of the entities in the higher planes) when channeling, is to be worked away from because it truly is coming from the channel himself. It is as memory tubes into the cells of the body. Each cell should be considered a mini-black hole, an inward bound vortex, pulling energy from above. This ability is there for people to draw on and help others. Do not misunderstand when it is said that it is truly the individual. They do get help and prompting at times from those on the other side, but the interpretation of most of what they get, when they do their writing and speaking, is coming from themselves and their background through many lifetimes, not just this lifetime.

In the future more people will be able to govern their own minds. Intense training in NLP (Neuro-Linguistic Training) would be of great benefit to those doing channeling. What it does is allow the channeling process to feed in while the everyday state is being maintained. This would be of great benefit to vocal channeling the proper way. Most vocal channels are not doing this. They are indeed in a trance, which is not the correct way. The proper function of the channel is to do unconscious receiving while talking to other people, using the material that comes in. This way it is much more relevant to the conversation that is taking place.

Remember, the present personality should not "vacate" the premises and give the body over to an entity on the other side. This is mediumship of the old age. The correct method involves not losing consciousness of the present personality, but stretching and strengthening the mind to allow the channeled beings "room," if you will, to join you in discussions and teaching sessions. When it is said that humanity is only using 10% to 15% of their brain, this is what the other 85% is available for, the knowledge and information of the creative channel. That knowledge and information should become part of us rather than allowing an isolated entity from out in space somewhere to come in and use our form.

When the teachers and guides send something through, it comes as a thought or thought-block. The channel then takes this and elaborates on it and interprets it (or misinterprets it) through their own personality. If the ego is still very strong they will twist and bend all information, all thought-blocks given to them. A thought is dropped down from the higher planes and it is there for anyone to pick up. It is not directed specifically to any one particular channel. The same thought-form is there for all to tap into if they are capable. Then it is interpreted or misinterpreted, whichever the case may be, by the personality of that individual. This is why channels must weigh all material that comes through and work away from naming names, because all they are doing is tapping into a thought-form which has been placed into the records by certain individuals. They are not truly contacting this individual. Let none tell you differently. The channel then elaborates on the thought-form they have contacted and this is where the coloring comes in.

Some Channeled Entities Themselves Are Into Glamour

Glamour is best described as anything that gives satisfaction to one's ego, a boost to their faltering sense of self-esteem. This is a pathetic situation for one with channeling capabilities to be caught in. Some entities on the higher planes that are being channeled are themselves into glamour. They were into glamour when they were on the earth plane and perhaps were making some progress on their own on the inner plane path until they started coming through someone on the earth plane. So you see, the ones on the earth plane that are channeling these entities are not only doing a disservice to themselves, but have also stopped and stunted the growth of the entity on the higher plane. Perhaps he is striving to right some attitudes he had that were very much against universal law. This is much harder to accomplish while on the inner planes and almost impossible for him to accomplish when fascinated with hanging around the one on the earth plane who is channeling him.

The more profound information for personal readings must come through a lower vibratory rate. Those on a higher vibratory rate cannot lower their vibration to gather the necessary information to satisfy the ego in humans without paying too large a price in energy drain. It simply is much easier for those on a lower level of evolution to do this type of thing. But some channels get "stuck" on this ring of energy far too long, and need to progress on, because time is always a consideration. There are compensations for moving on, even though they will be giving up the excitement of having people fawn over them because of the information they can provide. One of the compensations for moving on will be in dealing with the wisdom of the ages, not information to titillate and amuse their friends. The opportunities for their spiritual growth in this lifetime are phenomenal, but in most cases this growth is not taking place. Their emotional bodies are so badly out of harmony that it is pulling the rest of the form into disarray. They need to release the entity they are channeling, not only for his sake but for their own also. Some questions that I would like to ask them are:

- Do you not know that channeling this entity will cause trouble in your relationships?
- Do you not know that you need to progress to a higher plane of contact with the inner life?
- Do you not know that this will not, and cannot happen as long as you are locked into lower dimensional communication?
- Do you not know that there are different rings of energy each turning in opposite directions and that you need to move up to the next level as a start and even higher?
- Do you not know what your soul chose to do in this life?
- Do you not know that you cannot have balance when living with the conditions you find yourself in?

- Do you not know also that you cannot raise your consciousness level if the emotional body is not balanced?
- Do you not know also that you are in a perfect situation to strengthen this emotional body, if more time is diverted to spiritual study and contemplation?

Misuse of Power

Those who receive the gift of Holy Spirit, (the Holy Ghost or tapping into the rings of energy or the divine mind or whatever you want to call it) at the same time are endowed with much power to help humanity. It is a great responsibility and it's a very subtle thing to know when this power is being misused. Its misuse most often comes when this one is on the inner planes while sleeping at night. Therefore, if not in true contact in the waking hours with what took place during the night on the inner planes, then one does not realize that one is misusing it. When one's mind is tied up with day to day trivia it still can and must be free to apply incidents of third dimensional life to oneself. A good teacher must be able to come down and explain things on the level of the student. How else do you think those on the higher planes could teach us? We simply couldn't understand the concepts that they live their lives by. As an example, a good music teacher should be able, after a short interview, to know a new student's standing or level and immediately know what book or method this one needs to have and also what musical exercises. The same would be the goal in spiritual teachings. When teachings are just applied to the surface, they are not learned. Each piece of information needs to be absorbed and applied and worked with, until it either is accepted totally into the whole being as an unalterable truth for that one or it is utterly rejected

.

Conglomerate Channeling

True channeling, channeling done the correct way, the way that is to progress into the new millennium, will always have a conglomerate doing the transmitting, not one entity. An individual entity should not be using the form for his or her sole use. Now perhaps they are part of a conglomerate and only this one cares to be the spokesman, but this should be acknowledged if it is a fact. Most of those coming through singly have an ego problem and want center stage all to themselves.

Conglomerate channeling then meshes so well with the present personality (the person on the earth plane) that it takes someone with a good ear to detect when other facets of the present personality come into the scene. The more it is practiced, the smoother the process becomes, until there is no separation of thought or nuances in the speech. Once the synthesization has taken place, there should not be a distinctive difference between which member of the conglomerate the material comes from, and no difference between any of the three areas it comes from which are, remember, your own past incarnations, the teachers and guides and the universal mind. (Remember, this is the correct meaning of the Biblical term trinity – your trinity.)

The material is woven together in the computer of the mind and comes out as one unique line of communication from the channel. This is as it should be, as it must be. It can be no other way because our conglomerate cannot "take credit" for anything that is coming from our past incarnations because they had nothing to do with them.

Also, the conglomerate cannot "take credit" for how the channel interprets the universal mind. That also is the unique ability of the channel. And, naturally, they can't take much credit for what the channel has learned in this incarnation because even though some of the conglomerate may have been guiding the channel for part of this incarnation, the channel's experiences are uniquely their own. A conglomerate can take credit for, perhaps, one fourth of the material that issues forth from a channel and because there are usually seven in each conglomerate, each member of the conglomerate is responsible for only one-seventh of one-fourth of the material coming from a channel. Therefore, it does not make good common sense to put any of the names of those in the conglomerate on it. They are not interested in furthering who they were or what they were when they were on the earth plane. They are overjoyed that they can help all of humanity. This is the only answer that should come forth from any one working with the highest entities. This is the proper way for channeling to eventually evolve to.

Walk-Ins

A true case of walk-in is very rare and, believe it or not, is not a successful way of handling what it is that is to be accomplished. We are speaking of a soul who actually goes back to the inner planes and another soul takes over the human form. This is a "physical" walk-in and, as said, is very rare and not too successful. It is usually done by those of lower evolution.

The proper way for a master teacher to return to earth is by intertwining with the soul already in the human body in a "marriage" of spirit. This is highly successful. This is what took place with Master Jesus and many of the other great teachers. The entity who enters the form at birth is a "chela" or student of the master and brings the form up through the early years preparing it through education and nutrition to be able to handle the energy and to be able to understand the process of intertwining when it does take place. Many of the channels at the present time did not follow through with this process and now that the preordained time is upon them for the master to use the facilities, they cannot handle it and have many problems both physically and mentally. It has been said over and over again in these teachings that the arts are the saving grace of all humanity and most especially those who set the stage before incarnating to allow a master to use his human resources to enlighten humanity

Education through the Arts is Best Way to Open Channel

The most successful way of opening this creative channel in all will be by actual "hands on" creative expression every day of their life beginning at the youngest age possible. All must be encouraged to "express feelings" at all times. Perhaps theater is the best way for adults, because when they can pretend they are someone else, they can remove their vanity from the situation and express their feelings by hiding behind the character. The channel will open according to humility of the person, their motives for using it – which are known to those on the inner planes – and service to humanity, sincere service over a lengthy period of time. It also will open to those who have seen the pits of despair as far as their personal relationships are concerned. We are not saying that one needs to live in their own hell for a period of time, just that this does speed the opening. To sum it up, the creative arts are the best, safest, most sure and reliable way to open this channel in both children and adults. Every class the young child is in must be geared towards the expression of self.

After the opening of the channel is accomplished then all education needs to be aimed at the proper use and functioning of the channel – for instance, the energy that is needed for channeling. This is, of course, a progressive need and this is where education on nutrition needs to become an important part of training of the child at this time. There are certain foods and vitamins and minerals that will enhance the ability to channel and these nutrients need to be known and introduced into the diet at different stages of progress in channeling.

The individual goal for all is the totally synthesized man. The goal for humanity as a whole is the Brotherhood of Man. The first can only be reached through the creative arts which will lead to self-esteem for each individual, which will lead to the Brotherhood of Man. This is the middle path, the central channel, the balance point in all things and it must begin to be stressed in our school system.

Some Guidelines for Those Wanting to Learn to Channel

To begin with not all people chose to be able to channel in this lifetime. But for those who have a burning desire it most likely was part of their chosen plan of progress.

The simplest way to have people begin is to visualize the "other side" as something they are curious about and ponder on what the contact would be like – in other words, the field of energy that surrounds their inner being. As you start to channel and the realm of information that is needed goes outside the knowledge and experience of your inner being there is an opening of the channel that then allows access to higher realms of knowledge. In some cases your inner being must reach out into these other realms but in many cases the beings in the higher realms will come down to this opening. Depending on how spiritually advanced you and your inner being are, is what makes the difference. The more advanced you are, the higher up into the tighter vibrations this opening is.

Picture the energy being diffused around your physical body. The different layers of your aura each become progressively tightened up; as you reach up and expand out into the ethereal realm around you this tightening up continues. Your channel of communication progresses as your vibratory rate tightens up.

Therefore, the first thing that those wanting to channel must do is raise their physical vibration through perfecting their bodies. This is done with diet, exercise and health related massages, deep tissue massage, and spinal manipulation. Bio-energetics is another field that helps.

At the same time the vibratory rate of the mind must be tightened. This will be done by study of spiritual truths, meditation practices and clean thinking. No bad attitudes should interfere with positive thoughts. After a period of raising the vibration both inwardly and outwardly, which will take different times for each – for some it will be from several months up to perhaps several years – then comes the actual sitting down and concentrating on a question you have. It would be best if this question were one of general interest, not a personal question pertaining to some action you should or should not take. The reason for this is obvious. If it is a personal question, the personality will enter the picture and impress the mind with its desires, whether they are for the good of the entity or not. A personal question will contain the channel to the earth plane communication realm. A question of a general nature having to do with humanity as a whole will allow the inner being to need to open the channel to the higher realms. The beginning of channeling should focus on making that opening happen as soon as possible.

Many people at this time are channeling their higher beings and think they are channeling the divine mind. This is not so. They have contained the channel to the expertise of their inner beings but are not opening to abstract thoughts of the Creator. These abstract thoughts are what will stretch the mind.

Sometimes you will channel only your own inner being because this is the knowledge you are looking for at that particular time, but most of the time you will go right on past it and contact the universal mind. There are many stages of this universal mind and some of them come through as a single entity and some of them as a conglomerate. Many times it depends on what arrangements you made before incarnating as to what will be your point of contact. The most important thing is the desire to want to make contact and this desire must be for your own personal spiritual growth, not because you want to use the channeling as a gimmick at a party, etc. This kind of attitude will only draw unto you discarnate entities who will have fun with you.

The stage of pondering a question about creation, eternity or humanity as a whole is an esoteric stage and the information that comes will be almost poetic in nature and many times will not be understandable as a direct answer to what you were pondering. If you get a very specific answer with details, etc. you should immediately rule this out as true contact as you most likely have contacted a discarnate, and while they may not be using you to have fun with, this is not the level you want to tap into for spiritual growth.

This practice of pondering a question should take place each day, at the same time if possible, for a period of perhaps ten minutes to start. You do not go into meditation or make your mind blank. The doorway into the channel is through your own mind. Therefore, your own mind must be actively involved in the process of breaking through into the higher realms. This is where most people make their biggest mistake. They mistakenly believe they have to clear the mind and make it empty or go into a trance. This is not so. If it were so, everyone that does this sort of meditation would be channeling. The mind and thought processes of that mind must be involved. This mind is made up of your animal-based brain, your personality and your half of the soul on the earth plane. The contact is made with the half of your soul on the inner planes through magnetic attraction between the two halves of the soul.

When this contact is made the connection needs to have direction as far as what to do with the contact. This is where the personality comes in – using the transmitters of the animal-based brain to give direction to the connection. Once the connection between the two halves of your soul has a directed statement to respond to, then begins the process of stretching and reaching, if the information requested is outside of the half of your soul on the inner planes. This is why it should be a question of a general nature – a philosophical question. Otherwise the contact will stay at the earth plane level instead of opening the top of the channel to search outside of the soul's own experience. At this time, if proper preparation has been made and constant positive thought has been kept, you will contact the higher realms which are the true home of your inner being. Your inner being has, you might say, one foot in each of the two realms, the earth plane communication realm and the higher realms. This is why the questioning process is important as to subject matter. The earth plane realm is subject to influence and interference from earth bound discarnates and you must get past this stage.

Your first few attempts may only make it this far, and it is up to your common sense as to whether you think you are in contact with discarnates or higher beings. As given, it depends on your stage of evolution. Those not so highly evolved will reach discarnates who will then proceed to lead and guide a person into what this discarnate wanted to accomplish or finish in his life and didn't. This leads to all kinds of problems including mental illness, murderers, rapists, abusers and at times even leads a person to commit suicide. The inner being that you contact, your inner being, must be highly evolved enough to be able to shed these discarnates and proceed to step both feet back into the higher realms, but you must be wise enough yourself to follow your inner being even though it may not be as exciting or even as interesting as what some of the discarnates can tell you.

Chapter 3

THE FOUNTAIN OF KNOWLEDGE

"Neil, look at this picture of the fountain in a shopping mall we visited in Tucson, AZ several years ago. It always amazing to me that some of the water in a fountain goes higher than the rest. It seems to be at all different levels, but it's all coming from the same place," I said.

"Yeah, it sure is pretty," Neil replied.

Shopping Mall Fountain in Tucson

You know, of course that this reminds me of something the TimeTraveler talked about, don't you?" I asked.

37

"Yes, by now I know it does. What is it that it reminds you of this time?" Neil asked.

"When the TimeTraveler talked about channeling he compared it to different levels of a fountain that could be accessed at any time according to what you were curious about and wanted to learn more about," I answered. "Of course the fountain he was referring to had twelve levels and this picture only has three, but maybe that's appropriate anyway because this is where most people are at in their progress. Let's tune into the TimeTraveler and find out what he has to say about the comparison."

The Fountain or Rings of Energy are Inside Each

The rings of energy, the Divine Mind, I'm going to give a name once and for all – from here on it will be called the fountain. The layers or steps of this fountain, relate exactly to the levels of the mind. When people first start tapping in, it will be messages from dead relatives. This is level 3, and they move on up from there. The entity named Jesus was at level 4 when he was crucified.

This is usually the first stage of our 12 stage fountain that the beginning psychic taps into. Jesus Sananda, is no longer there, but His Akashic records are. He progressed on up the stages of the fountain and left records at each stage. When you continue on up in your inner spiral, you no longer contact that particular entity's records. What you do contact are the records of the entities who carried the spiritual banner at that particular time in the history of the planet.

The fountain inside you will be as a living history book, if you will, and can be used as such in your quest for knowledge of all kinds; the wisdom you must earn yourself. You can study either exoterically or esoterically and both ways at the same time, which would be using your divine heritage to the fullest.

Whatever a person is curious about, whatever he questions in his mind is what he will receive, because instead of "the fingers doing the walking through the yellow pages," the soul traverses the fountain and plugs into what the mind says it wants or needs to know. This should help bring home the fact that thoughts are things. The more control the soul has and the more contact established with it, the more profound information it will search for.

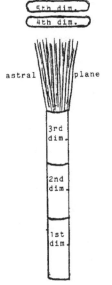

Rings of Energy Extending Up To Higher Planes

Picture a pipe in the ground standing up as high as you can reach with pressurized air coming out of it. On top of this pipe, floating on the air are many rings (flying saucers) or picture them as Frisbees, if you will. Between the pipe and the lowest Frisbee is a space consisting of just air, strong enough to support your heavy body. This is the astral zone that we have discussed previously.

The further up towards the bottom Frisbee, (level one of planet four) you go the less air pressure to hold you steady until you reach the security of the lowest Frisbee or plane four. As the fourth dimension has not many in it at present, you speed right up through it. You may linger long enough to get a glimpse of the next stage of fourth dimensional life, but there are none there to hold on to you. (Please keep in mind that I'm talking of your contact through your inner self.) This changes when you reach level one of planet five. Here you find your twin soul and can contact him easily. He is your guide for this incarnation and your progress then of being able to contact this ring of energy, this beam of Holy Spirit, if you will, is much easier from now on.

A computer must be programmed, remember, before it can do its seemingly miraculous work. Anyone wishing to perform miracles, as did Jesus, has only to desire this strongly enough to be able to direct the soul to tap into that exact level on the fountain. Anyone wondering about the pyramids, etc. needs to contact that exact level. Those that need to have verification of what they believe and desire it strongly enough for self-confidence will tap into the fountain at the exact level that is right for them.

So you see, not only does the personality need to have the guidance of the soul, (in other words, the animal brain needs to have the divine spark,) but also the soul needs to have the guidance of the personality, (the divine spark needs to be guided by the animal brain,) for the knowledge required to perform in today's world. Those who let the soul take total and complete control are not balanced. This is why opening chakras too soon is dangerous. Too much meditation is also dangerous as it keeps you in the day-dream state and not using your own intelligent mind.

Fountain of Knowledge also Fountain of Youth

Some people have trouble expressing emotions along with a lot of other people. I said expressing, not feeling. People sometimes feel these emotions, but fear to express them verbally. You don't need to express them verbally, but you can put them into some form of artistic release. Everyone is an artist of some sort. This is where the fountain comes in. You can use it to learn any new art form or to pull up from underground any art form you have learned from previous lives. Yes, this fountain must be pictured as the underground pipes being your previous incarnations. The water collecting at the base is your present life and as you go up each level or layer of that fountain, it becomes narrower and higher.

The fountain of knowledge that is inside each human being is also the fountain of youth. That was known in the Atlantean age and tales of it persisted clear through until the present day. There was a school with a series of classes in the Atlantean days that was attended by all and it was known as the Fountain of Youth. The Atlanteans were a very, very advanced civilization, beyond what you are capable of now on the earth plane, due to limitations which have been imposed from the higher dimensions, to slow the progress that did go the wrong direction in Atlantis. There is a method of braking controls in place now so that progress goes the right direction, because once the knowledge and enlightenment begins to come in it begins very swiftly to affect all. This is what happened in Atlantis. There were no controls in that time period to slow and correctly direct the energy and the power that the

Atlantians learned to tap into and then to misuse eventually.

Channeling and the Time Factor

The younger one is when they begin to channel, the less interference there is from the present lifetime, but the more interference there could be from previous lives, as a strong carry over from those previous lives. This would account for young people getting predictions about cataclysms, from remembering, perhaps even more so than an older person, what took place in a previous life. If this young person is a highly evolved soul with much knowledge of higher plane concepts available to him and has the ability at a young age to tap into the fountain, the creative channel, he should receive much good clear material unless it is colored and influenced by the environment around him that he finds himself in and the people with whom he is associated. This will then cause distortion.

This also accounts for the many predictions of cataclysms that are prevalent today. What is happening and going to happen is an inner replay of an outer display that took place in the past. This new beginning (the so-called New Age) is a returning of the ones saved – those who were lifted up and kept safe. The business of time and no time in the universe causes much trouble. The basic difference in some predictions is the fact that some entities coming in now remember only the information of destruction that was imminent at the time of the last cataclysms. Those who are not making these predictions, but are only preparing for a better world, are those who realize it has already happened and that they have been

42

returned to do what they were prepared to do in the time off the planet. In other words, the separation has already taken place and those who are predicting it now are those who were destroyed bodily and have come back in with memories of these previous times very strong in them. Those who are not predicting this are the ones who were removed and trained off the planet and are back to implement their teachings. The cataclysms have already happened! The New Creation talked of in the Bible is the same process that is ongoing now, the restructuring process mentioned as having taken place after the destruction of Atlantis. Time is irrelevant. It is all one and the same. (For more on cataclysms please see my book "Cataclysms?? A NEW Look at Earth Changes," published by Blue Star Productions of Phoenix, AZ and available through Amazon.com).

The information available through the creative channel is in a time order ring of energy, (the divine mind, the beam of Holy Spirit), and the time of those cataclysm messages is one of the easiest to be tapped into by beginning psychics. All have memories of those days of flooding and destruction and think they are seeing the future when really they are reading the past. This is why some people don't feel threatened as others do. They have been pulled past that time period on the pole of information and as they go higher they certainly understand more.

Cyclic Ebb and Flow of Channeling Needed

The new philosophy about channeling will concern itself with the individual right to grow and progress, each at their own speed. It will start with the schooling bringing forward the inner being of each person at a very early age.

This will lead to the necessary intertwining of this inner being with the present personality. This is most important. The direction that some are taking now is turning their whole incarnation over to their inner being. This is not what is wanted or needed. Can you imagine what the world would be like if all these inner beings were walking the face of the earth in embodiment? There would be no progress made because we would be stuck in outdated ideas for the most part.

The way the higher beings can help us is for us to be on the earth plane experimenting and sending them the results of our experiments. They then take all this material and condense it and come up with overview thoughts. These thoughts then are sent back to us for experimentation and this, then, returns to them. It is a cyclic ebb and flow of information that will progress the human race. If they were walking the earth with us or walking the earth by themselves it would not progress. It takes the one down here returning our thoughts to those up there. It was tried the other way and did not work. This was what Atlantis was all about. Since the restructuring of Atlantis, channeling has started opening in so many people that progress is much, much faster and becoming more so all the time. Eventually the channel will be wide open on children as they are born. This does not mean that they will remember their past lives; only that direct communication can be had with the channel in a momentary, cyclic process. This is the proper way to channel and is the proper goal for all

Questions from Readers

Question - How can I be sure when I meditate, that the messages and impressions I receive are from the "Star Buddies" or my subconscious?

Answer - When you meditate, you must then evaluate all "messages" or "information" you receive and then look at yourself honestly. Is what you are receiving always what you want to hear, similar to confirmation? If so, it probably is coming from your subconscious mind. If it is thoughts that "shake you up" and make you question your own concepts, it is most likely coming from the teachers and guides. Remember, please, that when just beginning to receive from this area that the teachers and guides will deal with personal problems to encourage you to continue. When the communication lines are stronger, then the material will become, at first, more profound for you personally, for your own growth and eventually it will become more meaningful to others as far as the growth of the rest of humanity. When this happens, the personal help will cease, for the most part for a period of time, until synthesization takes place between your higher and lower selves and then the personal guidance will be there at your fingertips at all times. It is a progressive path and the reasoning, intelligent mind must be applied to what you receive at all times. You must constantly ask yourself if it feels right or sounds right to you. This is what was meant by "testing the spirits."

Question - What percent of earth people are channels? What percent of those are highly evolved channels?

Answer - We would estimate that perhaps only one to two percent of all the people on earth are channels of anything other than their own past lives. Perhaps this is not what you meant. If so, we would guess that perhaps ten percent can channel from their own past lives. An additional one to two percent can channel the inner plane teachers and guides. We could not even put a percentage figure on those who channel the full range of possibilities such as this channel does. There are only five on the earth plane who can do this.

Summary

There is nothing unusual or spectacular or "of the devil" or harmful in channeling if it is understood as a perfectly natural process. It is the lack of understanding that causes problems. The greatest spiritual accomplishment anyone can aspire to on the earth plane is to learn to use their channel in a wise and loving way that is beneficial not only to themselves, but to all kingdoms.

Those who want to achieve this ability to channel must first transmute any attitudes they hold that are unbecoming to a God, as that is what they will become when the ability to channel their God Within becomes a reality. Therefore, this must be the first stage of progress for this channeling ability to open up. Transmutation of attitudes is the way to move on past the psychic stage. Transmutation is the bridge from each stage of the path to the next stage. There are always more bad attitudes of a higher level at the beginning of each stage that need to be transmuted. You go through a thorough transmutation process when bridging between psychic phenomena and channeling. You go through another set of transmutation of attitudes before the bonding takes place. Each set gets harder, but the seeker becomes more purified at each stage. The next set of attitudes for you to transmute would seem like very good qualities to those who are in the stage of transmutation between psychic ability and channeling. Even though you have achieved a goal to be desired, you know there are many higher and harder stages yet to come for you.

As given previously, there are inner spacemen and outer spacemen available to help humans on their spiritual journey. The inner spacemen are those who will be able to help direct and guide the spiritual path of the entities in incarnation on the earth plane. The outer spacemen are those from other planets who have the ability to be in direct communication with the people on the earth plane, but are not necessarily inclined to give information that will help further the spiritual progress of humans. They have no intentions of hurting them; they just do not have the understanding of the animal nature, including the emotional body of human beings. Humans are only partly of the same nature as these other planets and none from the other planets can ever fully understand humans and therefore are not able to truly help a human being. Their method of accomplishing spiritual growth cannot even approximate what a human must go through to accomplish this growth because they do not have an understanding of what it means to have evolved through nature the way the human being has evolved. The mere fact that human bodies are composed of material of which the earth is composed has much to do with the functioning of this body and the interaction of the body with the piece of the Creator which is embedded in each body.

Those from other planets have no conception of what it means to feel something in every fiber of their being. They only can approximate this feeling mentally, they cannot feel it. As they grow and progress they become much better at approximating these feelings. As they climb even higher they can offer much good advice from an intellectual standpoint and as they progress even more they can offer spiritual goals. They can explain their methods of reaching these goals, but they cannot ever really bring this down or relate this to what a human would have to accomplish in order to use the same methods.

Herein lies the problem of depending on help from other planets. They mean well for the most part, but truly are not as capable of helping as the inner spacemen. To explain what is meant by the inner spacemen, these inner spacemen are what is being referred to by other channels as your "inner being." This inner being that all humans have access to is a conglomerate of all thought that has ever taken place at any time throughout the history of the planet. This conglomerate inner being is not the divine mind, it is human mind condensed and compressed into only that which serves to further the growth and evolvement of human beings. There is an elaborate process that takes place with the thought-forms that stem forth from humanity. For the most part they are contained close in by the earth until they have been proven to be of absolute value as far as furthering the spiritual uplifting and uprising of the human spirit out of the animal flesh.

The thoughts that go forth are monitored and filtered into different conglomerates. These conglomerates are made up of previous personalities of those incarnated on the earth at this time. They take the current thoughts that are coming from humans and work with them and send them back to the humans who tap into this conglomerate mind. These humans take the thoughts and send them out through several different means such as books and lectures, to other humans. These other humans, in turn, have their own thoughts to add to or change what they read or hear, and these thoughts are automatically sent back to the conglomerate mind, or inner being, where they are once again monitored and filtered. These thought concepts that go through many periods of back and forth growth are what make up cycles in human history. They are also what are used to determine lessons that are to be worked on when a person begins a new incarnation.

This conglomerate or inner being of all humanity from time immemorial is the one, single most important factor or way of producing spiritual growth (and thereby fostering new stages in evolution) that is available to the earth planet. It has not been understood up until this time not even remotely by any. It is now time to further the understanding of how this works.

When a thought has been recycled to the point where it is an absolute principle for human growth and evolution it is then employed by those whose evolutionary growth is far enough along to be able to work with it. It is used to form future personalities on the inner planes who will have their opportunity to manifest at a later time as a spiritual master. In other words, the growth of masters who incarnate on the earth has been taking place for many thousands of years on the inner planes, which is the area of time/space continuum below the manifested level of vibrations. This is another area that needs to be explained. The vibrations below the manifested plane of vibratory rate are too strong to survive the transition that takes place when manifestation in the physical world comes about. This strength of vibrations is due to the difference between physical matter and ethereal matter. Ethereal matter is much closer to the original source of all vibrations, the Creator, and cannot, as given, survive the transition. Therefore, when one is working with using these strong vibrations and taking a perfected concept and wishing, then, to reincarnate and bring this concept into manifestation to teach it bodily to humans (instead of through thought processes) one must become this concept in the unmanifested state.

There is a definite way in which this is accomplished and the concept is sent through several previous incarnations as a partial basis for each incarnation building up, as it were, into one total lifetime of manifesting this concept on the earth plane. This buildup starts half way through the scale of vibratory rate that a spirit is working on and the lifetime as a master culminates on the lifetime of the twelfth tone of that particular entity's scale.

From my Teacher

This is the lifetime you (Norma) are in at this present time. As a master of creation, you have been working on these concepts for the last six lifetimes, embracing music in each one of these lives as the concept that one must become before manifesting and bringing this concept to humanity in manifestation instead of just through thought-forms.

It is necessary that everyone understand better how and when and why and where the most pertinent help for planet earth's inhabitants can and will and should come from. What I want to leave everyone with, is the fact that any information coming from outside the immediate area of planet earth will not be as applicable to humans in their struggle for growth as that which comes from the conglomerate mind that has been through all stages of evolution on earth thus far. This conglomerate mind understands what it means to be torn by betrayal, to feel lonely, to feel rejection and to feel constantly lacking in spiritual ability to communicate with the Creator. This conglomerate mind understands all this because these are the feelings that come through the emotional body of humans which is the flesh body that has evolved from nature out of the material of the earth.

Those from other planetary systems, such as the Pleiadians, can understand the wants and desires of the divine spark of those on earth and can give advice from this standpoint, but cannot give practical advice as to how to employ this advice and guidance when it must be used and filtered through and be embedded into the animal body that the spirits are embedded in. Without the wisdom of how to do this, the advice given by ones such as the Pleiadians are causing humans to feel that they can never be perfect and that it is futile to attempt to be something which they feel they are unable to live up to.

The perfection that the Pleiadians have as far as spiritual completion with their Creator can never be achieved by those on the earth plane. It is an impossibility due to the lowered vibratory rate of the human body, which is composed of material of the earth. Those from the Pleiades are of a much higher vibratory rate and never had a material body. Therefore, their advice and wisdom and knowledge is only confusing humans and causing a sense of dismay at their inability to become as perfect as the vibration from the Pleiades is. To begin with, this is not the goal for humans, to become perfection such as this. This is very far from the goal of humans. This is the danger of too much contact with other planetary systems. This all needs to be understood before this contact goes any further. Each planet in each solar system is serving an entirely different function from all others. There can be an exchange of information but there should be no pressure put on other planet's inhabitants to be exactly like any other planet.

To Recap

Balance is the answer in all things. If you sit around all day thinking of colored lights and "is my teacher trying to contact me?" etc., you are a candidate for Alzheimer's disease. Use your brain cells for goodness sake, if for nothing more than to figure out how to run a house more efficiently or find a better way to plant a garden; just to "build a better mouse trap" if you will, will keep the animal brain cells in use. This is why creative, artistic, releases are so valuable.

Chapter 4

FORMING THE RINGS OF ENERGY

"Here's a picture of the school both your Dad and I graduated from back in Ohio. It sure is a lot smaller than the one you graduated from in Grand Junction," I said to Neil.

School I attended in West Farmington, Ohio

"I had over 300 kids in my graduating class," Neil replied. "How many were in your class?" he asked.

"There were only twelve in my class. I think your Dad had about the same number in his," I answered.

"I guess it doesn't really matter how many were in each class, does it?" Neil responded.

"No," I said, "the schools still function the same way whether they're big or small," I answered. "The TimeTraveler had an interesting comparison to make between the grades in our schools and the planets we progress through on our spiritual journey," I continued.

"That sounds like an interesting comparison," Neil said. Let's tune into it."

"Okay, let's do it." I answered.

Grades in School Compared to Planets

In your schools it would be as if a child in the second grade is still considered to be of first grade accomplishments until he has completed that second grade. At that time is when he would be called a second grader. Those in the third grade are considered to be of second grade mentality until they have finished the third grade. This is the same thing that takes place on the planets. They're not even first dimensional until they have climbed through the twelve planes of the first planet and get to the ethereal body of the first planet before they are considered first dimensional.

You see, the spirit of each planet is found on the ethereal bodies of these planets. As an entity moves from the first to the second to the third he moves into the spirit, the ethereal body, before he is able to go on to the next planet. When he moves to the next planet he goes to the physical body of the planet and elevates himself, working his way up through the twelve levels of that planet and into the ethereal body, which then permits him to move on to the next. The same thing takes place there and that permits him to move on. Yes, each time, then, the entities work their way up through the twelve planes on each planet and into the ethereal body. Actually, the ethereal body is where that true dimension is. Therefore, the planet itself continues on the dimension previous to it.

When the guidelines for reentry for recirculation were tightened up, an entity had to attend classes and be schooled on the inner planes before he could reincarnate. These studies were guided by his other half. The halves that stayed up there did what they could to guide the ones who were in incarnation and these guides on the inner planes, then, were advised by the guides and the teachers from the other planets.

Planet Three

Slowly, through the centuries, we managed to build up very advanced humans who have formed their own ring of energy or ring of thought-forms. This comes about when an entity has perfected himself to the point that he no longer has to reincarnate on the earth. It took a long time for any to reach this. Just a few did. I, David, was one of the first ones to reach this point, Moses also. Most of the people in the early parts of the Bible were the earliest ones to reach this point because as they reached this point then they were able to send their thoughts back down to the others on the earth. They were able to contact them. Yes, in the way you're thinking, they were channeling and they would give their name. This is how the material in the Bible was given.

Eventually, these first ones would become mated with their twin and they stayed on the inner planes helping. They moved into the fifth plane with their twin and waited there and some of them are still waiting there for this pass of the Oversoul.

As they perfected themselves and did not have to recirculate, and then joined with their twin soul, they had the knowledge and wisdom of both halves of that twin so they are much wiser with a lot of experience to draw on. This is what entitled them, then, to go into rings of energy, bands of energy, which are in actuality, the spaceships. We have to bring this in; we have to talk about it, because humanity must begin to understand it. Before there were enough perfected humans, the rings of energy were the spaceships from outer space. The wheel that Ezekiel saw came from the circular shape of the ships.

The spaceships are in another dimension and vibrate at a higher speed. As we move into that fifth dimension we're no longer visible to those on the earth plane because those on the earth plane are only at the third level or dimension. They have not reached the fourth which they must because that was the third pass of the Oversoul. They have to make that jump, that climb into the fourth dimension before the fourth pass of the Oversoul can take place. That time is getting near for the fourth pass and those on the earth plane are not ready to go into the fourth dimension. This is why it has been stated that we will have to start creation over with the same type of destruction that took place in Atlantis, and only those more advanced and ready for the fourth dimension will be saved. Those who are not will go to the inner planes to be schooled until they are ready for that fourth dimension.

Planet Four

The fourth dimension is on the ethereal body of the earth and the same thing that takes place on the second and third planets also takes place on the fourth, the fourth being planet earth. You will not be considered fourth dimensional until you have climbed through the twelve levels of the fourth planet (Earth) and graduate into the fourth dimension ethereal form or body.

Planet Five (from David)

When we have perfected ourselves we move into the fifth planet which is Saturn. The energies on Saturn, the thought-forms, are in the band of energy around the planet. Let there be no doubt about this. This is where we are found and we stay there and circulate. It's like one big macro spaceship, if you want to picture it that way. This is the first ring of energy or satellite. Another term for a satellite would be a planet or a spaceship. This is what we want understood. It is very difficult because the material gets mixed up with the macro man and the micro man. The progression from the human standpoint of view, which is what you are when you are on the earth plane, is to this big planet Saturn, the macro universe. Then when we want to travel back to you, we become the micro men and this object that you view as a planet becomes a spaceship. This is very confusing. You can picture a ring of energy either way. This ring of energy can be said to be Saturn. This is where we all go when we're joined with our twin souls and we join that ring of energy around Saturn. This is the first stage of help back to planet earth, but on an individualistic basis. This would be the first ring of energy that you can tap into. When you tap into it in your inner being you need to think of it - you need to bring it down to your size. Picture us as micro men and picture that planet as a space ship which you can see inside your mind through your third eye. The functioning of your third eye opens up the two higher levels of your mind at that point. You can reach us from the second level, the second mind level.

To explain, your first mind level is the first, second and third planets, the second mind level is the fourth, fifth and sixth planets. Your first point of contact, of course, would be the fourth dimension, the very next plane above you, the very next level above you. But then you move on to the fifth and your contacts are with the sixth. Then when you go into seventh is where you can see us through the third eye and, yes, it was those from the seventh planet that you saw that night in your bedroom, Norma, because this is where your information, most of it in this time period, has been coming from, although since I, David, took over it has been coming from even above that. It has been coming from outside this solar system. I am spirit above the Oversoul's path, His twelve levels, so I am quite a ways above.

Records Left on Rungs of Ladder

As I, David, moved up through these rings of energy, I left records on the rungs of the ladder. I left records on the fifth dimension and as I moved out from the fifth dimension, through the last pass of the Oversoul and moved on to the sixth, I left records of more advanced knowledge on six. I moved on to seven and from seven on to eight, but from here on, our vibration is so high that it's quite difficult to come down and there are very few that can come back down. This is why this breakthrough with you is very highly unusual. We don't mean this to give you an ego problem; we're just stating it as a fact because it is unusual that there are seven of us that can reach back to you. This has not been possible earlier because there were not that many of us who are capable of it; besides you did not have that capability at that time. Your mission has all been planned that you reach this stage at the same point that we reached our stage, so that we could reach back and contact you and give this information, trying to explain humanity to themselves.

Now to get back to the ring of energy on planet five, we would like you to picture this as circular stair steps going up in the micro men stage of it. You also can still picture it from your point of view on earth as the macro stage of the planets growing bigger and higher, etc. Your first stage of contact would be the astral plane, the inner planes which are between the earth plane where they're still coming back to earth before going on to the fifth dimension. There are twelve levels of the astral plane. It's a reflection of the earth plane and when you first start to make contact, you receive good information because you reach the reflected plane which is a higher mental plane. But there is an area... picture it as in one of your wars what was called the demilitarized zone. There is a zone between the earth plane and the astral plane that is all garbled up. Your first point of contact is below that and then as you try to move up you have to work your way through this demilitarized zone, or the garbled zone until you come out on the other side of it into clear, pure contact with the pure rings of energy.

As you raise your own consciousness you can then contact the next plane up. Now I will still be there; I as David, who am above it all as spirit, have left records on the fifth plane that you can contact and tap into the wisdom and knowledge that I possessed at the time that I was there, but I am no longer there. You're contacting my records at that point. And the same thing happens as you move into the sixth and the seventh and the eighth and so on, right on up. You're behind me. You have to be behind me the exact number of generations that were between us from the time when I was on the earth plane until I no longer had to recirculate. Do you understand what I'm trying to say? I will always be that far ahead of you. That spacing will always be there. It's just like your birth years, your birth days on the earth plane. You can never catch up to someone who was born four years ahead of you or ten years ahead of you. That difference is always going to be there, and that difference will always be there on these rings of energy, this beam of Holy Spirit.

Planet Six

After we've perfected ourselves on the earth plane we are all together. To begin with, we have joined our twin and we are one whole complete soul. This is a beautiful feeling. You have no idea; you just can't imagine what a wonderful feeling this is going to be when it does happen. Not only are we joined with them, but we are then also joined in group consciousness, almost back together totally again as the Oversoul was before he split and went down to experience on the earth plane, which is a very difficult plane for the Oversoul. After that, when the Oversoul is all joined together on planet five, we move as the total Oversoul on to planet six where the Oversoul again shatters his sparks, but more gently than he did in the beginning on the earth plane and we do not split into two halves. We stay a whole complete spark.

This dimension is one of what you might call the occult blindness dimension because we cannot see or communicate with others. We have to be alone and plan for what we will do when we can progress to the next planet,

planet number seven. While on this sixth plane we are beautiful. We're whole, and totally beautiful. Our surroundings, our environment is totally beautiful with luscious trees, luscious fruit and luscious food. We are luscious, but there is no one to appreciate us and no one to discuss ideas or thoughts with. We're a thought-form and as thought-forms we have thought-formed ourselves into these beautiful bodies and we have all these beautiful thoughts, but as we said, there is no one to discuss them with.

But we do plan ideas that we think will help those behind us when we get to the point where we can reach back and help with more substantial help than the sixth planet can give. They can give some thought impression back, but it's just not as strong. It is much more individualistic type of thing. Let us put it this way – there is no conglomerate like you are in touch with now. When you get to planet seven is when two or three will join together, or even maybe five will start joining together, perhaps even the same other thought-forms that they joined with on planet two as ringlets of energy. And because they have similar ideas that they would like to pass back to humanity to try to help and they are interested in the same thing, they join together. We are also still talking spaceships, when you get right down to it, because we are micro men in these spaceships. This is the way we contact you, as we said, through the third eye. But at the same time, from the Oversoul's view, we are on the huge planet Venus. I'm afraid the more we talk about it, the more confusing it's going to be. You're almost going to have to keep a double picture in your mind or pretend that the planet Venus is the Mother Ship and we take the little ships out from there and come down to you. That perhaps would be the best way to state it.

Planet Seven

We then go on to planet seven where we have a very, busy, beautiful existence. This is probably the most beautiful of all planets in the crystalline white colors with overtones of lavender and purple. It is just absolutely a beautiful existence and we know that we are helping those behind us. This is the planet of help, number seven. This was my favorite and I stayed there probably longer than I needed to and I left considerable records on this planet.

Planet Eight

As we move on to planet eight...as you move up each one of these planets, you are reflecting up an octave higher in your vibration. If you want to picture it on your guitar perhaps, up until seven you have had the normal vibration pattern just getting faster and higher pitched each time, but when you go from seven to eight is when you go into a harmonic which is an overtone type of thing. For those who don't know music this may be hard to understand, but an overtone perhaps could be thought of more as an echo of the tone. It is so high and so refined that it has this hollow sound. From here on up then it is much, much harder to reach back because you're out in this echoing field, this dimension that is so refined. There are not that many who can do it. There are some.

Planet Nine

As you move from eight to nine there are even less and from nine to ten much, much less

.

Planet Ten

The ones on ten are not that concerned with direct one to one helping of those clear back on planet four. They're more concerned with helping those just behind them. The thoughts, the ideas from planet seven are the ones that those on planet ten wish to work with. This is the experimental station and this is where these thoughts will be tested and perfected, etc.

Planets Eleven and Twelve

From ten up to eleven and twelve there are very, very few that have gone this far. Earth is a fairly new planet and as in the beginning of the creation in your Bible, there was none from the earth plane to help any on the earth plane, so it is when you get to planet twelve, there is none from your own solar system that can help you, so your help then comes from a higher evolved solar system until you get enough to form your own help. This is the stage where I am at now, I am David and am above planet twelve, and I am one of the first to make it up here. When I say first, there are probably a couple hundred of us, but I was one of the first. This is where I am, on the ethereal body of planet twelve and I will, of course, leave a record here when I progress on into the mansion worlds. I will be done soon with the total solar system. We hope that it will not happen that you will lose touch with me because we hope that this contact can stay open as I progress on into the mansion worlds to reach back, giving explanations of these worlds to those back where you are at. If, when I make this final step forward, you make a step forward at the same time, then you will, in turn, pass this information to those before you and at the same time leave a record at the point on the Akashic records where you are at when you receive the information back from me.

We will start now to focus in, center right in more on planet earth, both the third and then we will go into the coming fourth dimension which everybody is trying, should be trying to reach. This is David signing off.

Rings of Energy are Space Ships

When we speak of higher rings of energy and conglomerates and planes and realms, etc., it is space ships in your language. There are seven in our ship and we are the ring of energy you are in contact with. Of course we can patch you through to a higher ship. When we say we are going to take you higher to get some information that is what we mean. We don't want to frighten people off, so have not spoken recently of this, but people must accept the truth of their divine inheritance. We are your elder brothers. You are our colony, our experiment, and you, Norma, were sent down in the seventh landing to be our communicator.

A person begins each incarnation by choosing goals and then choosing strengths you have gained in previous lifetimes to help you reach these goals. These strengths are the points of contact you make esoterically – your previous incarnations that you chose to help this one. These are what are released when you reach the stage of evolution necessary to cause your "rebirth into continuity" (born again) to take place.

When each entity perfects his soul to the point of not having to reincarnate again; when he moves into the realm of true spirit, he is indeed in an energy form. This energy form is a "thought-form," but a conglomerate "thought-form." This is to say that it is the experiences, intelligence and wisdom of many, joined together into what we term "rings of energy."

These rings of energy usually have about twenty entities in manifestation to five on the inner planes. This is a rough estimate; there is no set amount you see, as it depends on the evolutionary standing of those on the earth plane. There could be a ratio of five to two hundred, or five to four hundred or even higher, but five to twenty is more the normal. There will never be less than five in each ring, but seven is also a common figure.

The vibrations making up these pools of energy are the accumulated totals of the lifetimes of those in each ring. This is a stage of the inner life lesson plan that all partake of at a certain point in their evolution. We can serve in the area we choose, within certain limitations, depending on our level of development and expertise.

The seven of us involved in giving this material have multi-faceted lifetimes to draw from. Some of us have been rapscallions and some angelic beings at one phase. This is possible, to come back down to more effectively serve humanity. This is what several of us are doing at the moment, while some of us are still on the upward spiral. There are progressions made by us in these rings of energy. As we said, some of us have even descended to do this work

Rings Hold Meetings

At times there is a joining of many rings into one big circle. This is once a month at the full moon for a limited group to join, and once a year for all to join. These are necessary meetings for us, to hand out promotions and receive inspiring lectures and discuss problems and generally enjoy the comradeship.

True, there is no time here as such, but there is a rhythm and this rhythm determines the meetings. We just know; we feel or sense it is the right rhythm. We do join rings according to levels of development. It would be at the monthly meetings as though everyone in all first grades in a city school system, who had been holding hands in a circle in their own classroom, split their hands apart and joined in a circle with all the first grades. The yearly full moon meetings would involve the first six grades all joining and the upper six all joining. They would never all twelve join. We believe this way of meeting could be applied to schools on the earth plane for purposes of promotions, lectures, etc. and should be done on a regular basis.

God is Embodied in Rings of Energy

This is just some information that we thought would make us seem more real and reachable to those in incarnation. This is the revelation that the Christ wants understood in this time-frame of evolution. Humanity needs to understand this concept. It is part of the awareness that must come – that God is not a huge father figure sitting on a throne up in space. He is embodied in these rings of energy for your benefit. This is His only way of being able to reach out and help all humanity at one time. This concept must be realized by humanity before the next step can be taken.

If people could picture what we are talking about with these rings of energy, these rings of lights; if they could see what they feel they have to call "God" as this circle of energies that have grouped – then perhaps they could better work with the energies or, if you will, "cooperate with the will of God."

The answer to the question as to what is right when receiving conflicting answers from different channels, must be the quality of the answer from the standpoint of the reasoning, intelligent mind, and remember, that what seems and feels right to you will not to another. That is why you have free will to believe what you want to believe.

The difference in the material coming from different channels depends on which ring of energy they have tapped into. You see, you can have the ability to tap into this ring at any level. Those committing evil deeds are very capable of easily tapping into higher rings with the proper education as to what they are doing. They, the ones doing evil, are tapping into plane two, most likely the higher end of plane two, or the lower end of plane three, and they get caught there due to pleasures and excitement that they find. Some feel very comforted by what they find here on plane three, which is the plane the churches will be found on, and fear to step off this ring and move into what they consider uncharted waters. There are some who move past this third plane who think they have all the answers, are satisfied, and this is the end of their progress for that incarnation.

Rings of Energy Compared to a Kettle of Soup

The new revelation that the Christ, Lord Maitreya, feels it is time to discuss – that of God as a grease puddle of energy – is going to go against the grain of many, but this is the best comparison we can make. Picture a kettle of soup. There are many rings or puddles of grease on the top. Some are big, some are small. As grease continues to rise to the top in minute pieces, it gravitates to one certain grease puddle and clings there. Picture each puddle as having a different color perhaps and the color coming to the top goes to the exact same color as it is. These different colors are different areas of interest and expertise when making the transition to picturing God this way. He is many different grease puddles up on top of the soup.

Healing needs to be done by the concrete mind for the physical body, but healing of the ethereal body must come from the universal mind, which is higher and more powerful and all-inclusive than the grease puddles. Picture the universal mind as the kitchen the pot of soup is cooking in. This kitchen has the smell and feel of everything that has ever taken place in any kitchen anywhere in the world from the beginning of life. This will give you an idea of the universal mind. This is the source that must be tapped into to heal the ethereal body, which must be healed before the concrete mind can then heal the physical.

The grease puddles of energy are to help step down the healing from the universal mind on the ethereal body to the concrete mind to heal the physical. They are the go-betweens to correlate what one needs to have from one source and filter it to the other source. This is where the saying Father, Son and Holy Ghost came into being. This was the way one communicator interpreted the knowledge he tapped into, instead of a kitchen (Holy Ghost), a kettle of soup (Father) and a grease blob (Son). The Holy Ghost is the kitchen in our analogy and The Father is the kettle of soup and the Son is the grease blob. Just remember that all of it is energy!

When one below raises his consciousness enough to rise up (in his thinking), he comes into contact with a certain grease puddle that then becomes his "pool" of teachers and guides. As far as names for the channeling, we believe it would be better to call it Holy Spirit, as this is what it is. It will not always be any particular name. It is a conglomerate that is being channeled. We will keep giving it names if humanity insists, but would like to work away from this format, as this can become a circus, a farce, if allowed to continue. We believe it should be termed spirit or source or mind or intelligence or conglomerate or rings of energy or grease puddles – anything except the name of a real entity. You do not need to distinguish between us, because we are all one mind as far as the information being transmitted and as far as our guidance and protection of those in our charge. Think of us as a conglomerate, because that is what we are. We are one ring of energy, or light if you will, that is tuned to the exact vibration of those we are helping on the earth plane.

Chapter 5

TEACHERS AND GUIDES LIKE CLIMBING STAIRWAY

"Look at this picture of all of us (Neil's family and I) on the steps of the capital building in Denver," I said to Neil as we continued to clean up the picture files on my computer.

Norma, Fiorella, Claudia & Neil

"Do you remember why we took that picture?" Neil asked. Without waiting for me to answer he continued, "That shiny plaque on the step below us indicates where the mile marker is because Denver is known as the "mile high" city. From what I understand the marker has to be moved every so often from one step to another because the geology of the area keeps changing," he continued.

"That was really interesting, wasn't it?" I said. "Stairs are all really very interesting things, you know," I said. "There are all kinds of stairways, each suited for exactly what it is needed for," I continued.

"I know – now you're going to use it to lead into something the TimeTraveler talked about," Neil said.

"You got it," I replied. "He compares climbing stairs to the teachers and guides we contact when we meditate. Would you like to hear more?" I asked.

"Yes, I would. It will be interesting to hear what he has to say about that," Neil replied.

Teachers and Guides Compared to Stairway

We would like to discuss further the so-called teachers and guides that one reaches when meditating. It is like climbing a stairway. As spoken of before, these stairs are not flat steps; they must be pictured as rings of energy. Each ring is turning a different direction as you climb. If people can relate better when putting a name on each circle, each step of the stairway, then let them. They really and truly are bands of energy arising from the earth plane that can be tapped into. Everyone has the power to tap into this stream of knowledge. When they do, they tap into the lowest level and they must work very hard to get up any higher, and they must continue working, they can't just stop. The same words are up here for anyone to reach if their vibration is high enough. This source can be tapped into in times of stress or crisis.

Each Step Up Reflects an Octave Higher

This is very difficult to try to explain to those trapped on the earth plane. The overall pathway or stairway, if you will, can be related in your mind as to what you have always heard of as the Holy Spirit. Another term would be Divine Mind. As this stairway progresses higher and higher we can relate this to music because each band, each ring of energy, reflects up an octave. Remember our discussion of a guitar as a good illustration. As it jumps its octave, it gives off harmonics; it reflects an octave higher. This is precisely what happens when you advance on these rings of energy.

These rings of energy can be related to the religious teachers and figures throughout the Bible. When the first matings were done, when the first sparks of the Divine Mind entered the bodies of animals, there was no Holy Spirit to speak of above the earth. It had to be built. As these first entities passed on they went up, the spirits arose and this plane was built in this manner. Now this is not the astral plane, this is not the inner planes you go to between incarnations. We're talking above that. The astral plane is backwards, remember, because it is a reflection of the earth plane. The higher planes that we are discussing are above that. These are the emotional, mental and spiritual levels and above. Each level is one of those harmonics, one of those octave higher jumps in progression. The religious leaders spoken of throughout the Bible and in other countries, in other civilizations referred to by names not appearing in the Bible, are simply labels on these stair steps, depending on what level they were at as far as what name they were incarnated under at that time. This is very difficult.

We are going to use your own case, Norma, as an example to simplify the task of explaining. When you started your writing you merely were reaching parts of yourself, former incarnations of your own self. As it continued and refined, you did tap into the closest level, I will not say the lowest level, but the closest level in time; time and space being as one. The last person on the earth plane to have tapped into this energy and to have been well remembered, as having received this Holy Spirit, was the man known to you as Jesus the Christ. Therefore, the first stairway you tapped into, if you so desire to call a ring of energy a stairway, was the one known as Jesus. As you continued your writing it did climb higher, and you jumped to the next level.

As You Climb Up the Stairs You Go Backwards in Time

At one point in there you had been in contact with the man known as Joseph. Going back in an earthly family tree, Joseph would have been before Jesus. You progressed up that family tree in your receiving, and you reached the level of energy or step that is where King David was when he was on the earth plane. He was in contact with the Holy Spirit at that level. This is the level you contacted him (David) at. He is no longer on that level; he has progressed onward as you must progress onward. And as you do progress onwards, these harmonics will keep growing higher and higher, and fainter and fainter and smaller and

74

smaller, until they disappear into that black hole known as the central core, the Divine Mind.

This is the goal; this is home for all humanity. Once it reaches the central core, once it reaches "home," it is cleansed, purified and its knowledge synthesized into the Divine Mind. Then it is recirculated again into a different experience, a new solar system that is just being created and you help create it and build it and perfect it. We do not want to go any further on with this at this time, because this knowledge is really past the understanding of most of your seekers in the world today, but this will give you some idea perhaps of the total pathway for this particular solar system.

Shouldn't Get Stuck On Any Ring of Energy

There are many different planes that can be tapped into. Getting stuck on one ring of energy can retard your growth. You will need to keep moving on to higher rings of energy as you progress and evolve. Until you send out thoughts on a certain subject, you will not receive information on it. If you send out only shallow thoughts, you will receive shallow information in return. You need to send out more profound, astute thoughts and more profound information will come back to you. You must program your own computer. If you want to be a "master," you can be. The information on any subject is up here. What you do with it determines your growth and fulfillment.

As you continue channeling it is your mind that is reaching these levels. As spoken of before, if you want to put a label or name on each step then do it. But remember, it is this beam of Holy Spirit, a circular stairway, how else can we put it, that you are ascending. As you climb these stairs, there are fewer and fewer on these steps, which means there are fewer and fewer past experiences to tap into. Only the good experiences are stored under the ethereal name on the Akashic records and this is what you are tapping into.

As you move up in this beam of light, this Holy Spirit, this ray, this energy field, you will go backwards on the family tree, the line of communication will go higher and be lighter and smaller and dimmer, and you will eventually reach those who were the ones who inseminated the animals with their genes to help humanity on the earth plane. The further back you go, the closer the energy gets to the truths of the Divine Mind. As it gets closer, it gets purer; it is not as contaminated and muddied with error.

Astral Plane Entities have Large Bodies

Those on the astral plane waiting for the opportunity to reenter the earth plane have large bodies or forms, similar in size to what they had while in incarnation only, of course, these bodies are of ethereal matter. They can also influence those in incarnation and do, but usually only as far as day to day matters go. They have neither the depth of wisdom nor the overview necessary to give long term help and guidance. Most of them will not harm you unless they were that kind of person while on the earth plane. As many different kinds of people there are on the earth is how many different kinds there are on the astral plane. As there are people on the earth of a makeup that can commit heinous crimes, so also are there the same kind on the astral plane. This is why this stage of receiving must be progressed through swiftly – so you move out of the influence of this kind.

These in the astral form cannot enter into the thought processes and be seen as tiny humans through the inner eye. They can be seen through the outer eyes, and will be seen full size as a wispy figure – more like a cloud. They simply aren't perfected enough to pull the diffused energy around them together into a neat, compact ball of light that those who have perfected themselves become.

When the perfected beings want to enter earth's aura, they become diffused and wispy also because this is the result of lowering the vibration. Most of them do not care to be seen this way and will only do it under extreme emergency as it takes a toll on their energy field and delays their becoming micro men again to more intelligently help humanity.

Once above the seventh plane, there is a marked difference in the vibrational rate, a huge jump between the seventh and eighth planes that makes it difficult to go backwards. Some overcome this and occasionally do go down, but very few do. This is why most reaching back is done from level seven.

There is Constant Movement of Spirits between Planes

Fine lines must be drawn between the levels of each plane, but they truly are in a state of ebb and flow. There is a constant motion of spirits circulating between planes. It is similar to earth. You are in touch with those on many different levels of evolution. You can't just say that you'll deal with no one who is not on the same exact level as you are. We must live with and interact with those on any level.

So it is on the inner planes. True, the ones above the seventh plane usually do not and this would be true also on earth as these ones rarely reincarnate. A very few do at times. The entity known as Jesus was one of the few, Confucius another. These ones that do are very, very good at lowering their vibration enough to mingle and interact with those of lower vibrations.

The seed core has the capacity to spin off one hundred and forty-four probable realities. Until this seed core has used itself up, it stays on the earth plane. The probable realities already used (past incarnations) wait on the fifth, sixth and seventh planets. Then all are gathered back into one seed core (Oversoul) and finish the journey in this solar system, eighth, ninth, tenth, eleventh, and twelfth planets, as a complete Oversoul with the knowledge that all one hundred and forty-four realities gained for the Oversoul through planets four, five, six and seven. The spacemen from Venus, the seventh planet (plane) still have five more planets to progress through before leaving this galaxy.

Micro Men

A Micro Man is what you become after you have perfected yourself to the point where you no longer have to incarnate on the earth. You become capable of entering and influencing individuals who are incarnated on the earth plane and also those on the astral plane.

To explain, Macro-Man was whole. Each entity was a part of the whole. They were comparable to one drop of water in an ocean of water, or currents of electrical energy that were blended into one huge energy field. Then the sparks of electrical energy were split in half. After this takes place each half works on itself (by incarnating on the earth plane) and is synthesized in his or her own right. Then they are joined back into one whole complete divine spark that joins the immense energy field from which it came. Now it is a more individualistic part of that energy field, a part that has wisdom and knowledge peculiar only to that particular spark. This is when he becomes a Micro-Man, one tiny drop of water in an ocean of water – so infinitesimal as to be invisible. But this Micro-Man can be pulled out of the stream of water, or the energy field, and individualized again with his particular knowledge.

You see, the large macro mind (God) cannot get a proper perspective of the individual planets unless He can condense Himself. He does this by infiltrating the minds of humans. The human then, by inner contact with the God Within through the creative channel, can gain a perspective of the large macro universe which he is too small to experience in its totality – the same way God was too large to experience the small planets until He shattered Himself.

Rebirth into Continuity

As God shattered Himself into individual sparks and entered human bodies, so also does the human, at the same stage in evolution, shatter himself. This shattering releases the human's former incarnations to enter the bodies of Micro Men, who are the teachers and guides of our inner contact. An entities' former incarnations are in time and space and, up until this shattering, are in a vacuum inside the mind of the human. The shattering allows them to take form and rise up and expand into the universe. It frees all the knowledge and wisdom gained in these other lives, making them available for others to use.

This also begins the growing and evolving process for these past incarnations. This is the true meaning of the term to be "born again" for which the correct wording is a "Rebirth into Continuity."

These previous incarnations, our own and those of others, are the Micro Men that we contact when channeling. They are the inner and outer spacemen which, in reality, are the inner selves of humans expressing in an outward manner what they are not able to express, due to oppression, on the earth plane. Channeling is of great spiritual importance as the human cannot progress in spiritual growth until it is accomplished. Channeling has a direct relationship with UFO's in that the sighting of a UFO is a spiritual experience that is directly connected with an entities' ability to channel the higher mind dimension & planets. It is an event that can take place either exoterically or esoterically and is cause for celebration because it is confirmation that the rebirth has occurred.

The Splitting of the Atom

It all started with the splitting of an atom, which split again and again and again on an ever decreasing size scale (the nuclear reaction at the time of the "big bang"). You are a cell, one tiny cell, in the body of the Creator. You are to the Creator in the exact same relationship as one of the cells in your body is to you. Your body and its recirculating of the blood and cells is a direct repeat of the process of the Oversoul, who is a repeat of the spirit who is a repeat of the Creator God who is a repeat of the Central Core. If your cells run wild, there is disease. If enough of your cells run wild the total body, the physical form, is annihilated but not the mind. It continues to live. Therefore, if the earth were annihilated the Creator would continue to live even though His physical form were destroyed.

From my Teacher

The splitting of the atom is exactly what it is, with the Central Core the smallest, but at the same time the largest, most encompassing part. It is the smallest because of compressed time and space. As you leave the reality of the earth plane and progress onward, you become infinitesimal. We, as we are now, Micro Men, if you will, are infinitesimal and as we materialize onto your plane of existence we become gradually larger as though coming out of the point of a pin. When we speak through you it takes much of your own energy because you have to magnify the "voice" of one who is as tiny as a pin prick, to the degree of volume necessary to be heard as normal by you. This is why your vibration needs to be increased, so you can do this magnification. As you learn to do this, to be able to speak it, you are also helping to be able to see us.

We are from a different dimension. It is all a matter of vibratory rate. When you can raise your vibration high enough you'll be able to see us. You, Norma, have raised it high enough to hear us and feel us, but sight takes a higher level of purification of lower frequency vibrations. There are many ways to achieve this. It has to be a triple effort on the part of all three bodies; the physical through food intake and physical locomotion exercises, specific physical exercises, mental purification of thought and specific mental exercises, and emotional control which will come as a result of the other two. We are directly above you at the moment. When you feel energy, it is us. When it makes you ill there is more than one of us. You need to purify your body to not become ill.

When you see us in your mind's eye, the third eye, you see us as complete, do you not, but so tiny as to be inside that third eye? To bring us to manifestation you need to let us grow up out of the black hole of the third eye and become as large as life – as large as you. Those who see us are able to do this almost automatically. The third eye will be opening in many more people soon. Those who can't see us yet need to work on it more.

Subatomic Particles make up DNA for Humans

Subatomic particles are pieces of the Creator. You have more than one in your body; you have many. Each individual has a different number based on their evolutionary progress. The same is true of atoms which are a conglomerate, or collection, of the subatomic particles. These are that which make up the chromosomes and determine the coding of the DNA for each individual. It is the goal in the Science of Biology, as found in The Science of Music, to show humankind the way of determining the amounts of subatomic and atomic particles in each form. It is in these numbers that the causes and cures of disease lie. This will all tie in, of course, with the Healing Machine when all of the Science of Music is pulled together into one beautiful composition of the Harmony of the Spheres, which will be total perfectness of the Creator.

The entering entity is made up of subatomic particles as being his "piece of the divine" that we speak about. The physical form is made up of atomic material; the entering soul is made up of subatomic material. Maybe this statement will shed some light on the correlation.

82

Micro Men are Cells in Your Body

Not every subatomic particle in the body on earth will have a life on another planet. There are many cells in the body all made up of subatomic particles, but not evolved subatomic particles. In most human beings the past lives are locked into suspended animation as far as being inside the brain. They have their own life on the big planets but are not able to be seen on the TV screen of the person whose seedcore they are a part of. They are in the seedcore and are actively studying, growing, traveling, communicating and planning – in other words, living a life actively on other planets. They are not available as a selection of the dial of the incarnated person's TV until this person activates them by stretching and growing exoterically. This would be the approach to the first stage of synthesization. At that time, then, they have the double life, but it is only the subatomic particles that have been a part of previous lives – and that are used as part of the physical form make-up this time – that have this double life.

In the exact same way that you cannot be considered a cell in the body of the Creator until you have activated your past lives, these cells cannot live a life on an individual planet while serving in the physical body. They have the instinct of the lower kingdoms but not the reasoning capacity of the upper kingdoms until the person whose body they are in makes the breakthrough into releasing past incarnations, their "Rebirth into Continuity." At this point the cells of all parts of the body become activated and the animal instinct begins to withdraw and be replaced with "God Substance." This is part of the evolution of

83

subatomic particles. When this happens these cells then have the potential of evolving to the point of being Micro Men and someday being able to have the dual life, but not until they have served in many physical bodies in a higher evolved capacity each time, with the brain cells of the animal-based brain being the highest stage of physical evolution. At the next try at entering the body they will transmute into a Micro Man to be used only by divine will as a member of a past life that has accomplished the supreme stage of growth for his kingdom and does not have to return to physical bodies. He will now be free to serve in the capacity of early standing Micro Men. What this means is that once the physical family tree he belongs to makes the rebirth by an incarnated entity, he will become alive and part of that brain, even though he also has his own life.

From my Teacher

Compare it to a person being an active and alive member of an organization or work force. He is on the job for a certain amount of time each day, and then is free to go home and be with his family. The same is true with us. When we are at work we are in Norma's brain, when not on duty we are on our home planets. The same way a member of a work force can be called out at night in an emergency, so are we always available. You use the telephone; we use instant communication or ESP, if you will.

The evolution of subatomic particles follows the same pattern as the evolution of humans and planets, just a different size scale. While we are in Norma's brain our minds can travel to our home planet the same way as when one of you humans are at work your mind can travel to your home. If a bond is strong enough you can even have instant communication mentally with one at home. We can do this at all times because our total way of communicating is by mental telepathy. When traveling between our home planet and Norma's brain, it is done instantaneously by light waves, or radio beams if you wish, but totally instantaneously. Therefore, we are available immediately if there is no interference in the radio wave transmission.

When a channel's physical body is out of balance there is usually interference in the radio waves that we use for travel. While on our own planets we are of a size scale that is comparable to your size scale in relation to your planet. We must condense ourselves to tiny little Micro Men to ride the waves of space at the speed that we do. We have said in the past that your spaceships were too large in size and this is partially what was meant by that.

Chapter 6

MY PERSONAL EXPERIENCES

"You know, Neil, a lot of people ask me how all this started with me," I said. "That made me start thinking that maybe I should document it so others could see how it took place."

"That sounds like a good idea to me," Neil replied. "Why don't you get started on it? Meanwhile I'll continue looking through my pictures for flowers to use in your Flower Collection Songbooks. Say, what about using this as a cover picture for the Columbine Collection Songbook, songs about Colorado?" Neil asked.

The Columbine – Colorado's State Flower

"That would be great for the cover. We could make the title the same color as the flower," I said excitedly. "Getting back to what I was talking about, I really like to read about other people's experiences, so most of the reading I do is either autobiographies or biographies. I'm interested in what happened to them – what events took place in their life to bring them to moments of fame and fortune. I think it's all very interesting," I continued.

"Yes, I kind of like them too," Neil responded. "For instance, in my case being a computer scientist, I've always been interested in how Bill Gates got started in his career. I haven't actually read about him yet, but it's on my list of to-dos."

"I'm going to start trying to write my memories of how I got started in metaphysics. I think the TimeTraveler will be able to help me," I said.

"Go for it." Neil replied.

My Fiftieth Birthday

When I got up on the morning of my fiftieth birthday I decided to celebrate by giving myself the day to do anything I wanted – something that I had always wanted to try and had never allowed myself time to do. I decided to try to write music. It seems unbelievable that I had been playing piano since the age of four and had never tried to write music on my own. It just never entered my head that I would be able to do this. I didn't believe I was intelligent enough.

I did not particularly like the first song I wrote. It was titled "Walk, Walk, Walk with the Angels," and I couldn't believe I had written it because I wasn't especially religious – in fact, I was not religious at all. I was a church organist in a paid position and had been for many years in many different denominations of churches. I was always left with the feeling of not being able to believe what all those other people professed to believe.

I shrugged this song off, a little disappointed in myself and tried again. The next one was called "Elisa" and was about a girl singer I knew. This song had several verses and was a very true picture of her. The next one was "Daddy was a Bootlegger" which was about my father and my family and was also based on true facts. The last one I wrote that first day was "When the Columbine Turns Blue Again" and at the time I didn't know what prompted it. It was set in the mountains where we went to cut firewood at times and the columbine (the state flower of Colorado) would be blooming, so was based on true fact in a way, but I couldn't figure out where the words came from. As I look back now, it seems to be about the other half of my soul that, of course, I had to leave when I incarnated this time.

My Life in Ohio

As a matter of fact, I can remember as a little girl, perhaps five or six, wondering where my twin brother was and when I was going to be able to see him. I called him Norman and told my older sister about him – that I had a twin brother. She, of course, laughed at me.

As I look back on my childhood and early adulthood, there were many things that I took for granted that seemed strange or out of place, to others. For instance, in elementary school, perhaps fifth or sixth grade, we had to write a story for English class. I wrote one about "juke joints," which I realize now described the 50's scene exactly, as far as teenage hangouts. This would have been written about 1939 or 1940.

It seems I never did anything at the time that others did it as far as society was concerned. I entered first grade at the age of four and graduated from high school at the age of sixteen. Ten years later I entered college. I did manage to get married at about the same time as most other girls of my generation did, at the age of nineteen, but I was thirty-nine when my first and only child, a son Neil, was born. Now here I was at the age of fifty beginning to write music. Unbeknownst to me at the time, I would leave home at the age of fifty-seven with $60.00 in my pocket to eventually move to California and start a new business.

But I'm getting ahead of my story. After I was married I kept wondering when my life was really going to start. I was interested in psychic phenomena, but scared of it at the same time. A friend wanted me to go with her to a psychic for a reading and I wouldn't go. One New Year's Eve, this same friend had a party at her house and after playing a dance job that night, my husband and I went to her party. They were playing with the Ouija board when we arrived about 3:30 am and I joined them. My husband was not interested in anything like that and wouldn't join us. My friend asked the board when and if I was ever going to have children. We had been married about fifteen years at this time and had not been able to have children. Everyone laughed and they laughed even harder when the board said that yes, we would have a son. Five years later we had a son.

My younger sister and I used to experiment with ESP. We would set up a situation, such as I would sit and look at a Christmas catalog and my sister would concentrate on me and then call me and tell me what she saw. She saw me addressing Christmas cards. We were right so many times that we began to feel we were invading the other one's privacy and eventually quit.

My uncle would come over and bring a pendulum and ESP cards and we'd experiment also. About this time my older sister started doing automatic writing and an entity named Seth came through occasionally. I kept after her to quit; I told her that it was dangerous. She wrote some very nice prose at this time, but one day the entity coming through her threw the pen she was using across the room. She got scared and quit and now she ridicules me for what I am doing. I tried automatic writing years later in Colorado. The first legible message I received was, "This is Mother Hickox." I didn't know if it was my husband's mother or his grandmother because I knew them both by that name, but the incident did scare me and I quit trying to do automatic writing.

The next strange thing I can recall was while in church one day playing a communion service, I looked up at the people coming down the center aisle to the altar and there was my mother-in-law who had passed away about six months before that. She was wearing a green dress that I had made for her to wear at her youngest daughter's wedding. I couldn't believe my eyes, but there she was. I had to look back at the music I was playing and when I looked up again she was gone.

Several years after this my husband's younger brother was very ill with cancer and I would stay with him all night in the hospital because one member of the family was always with him. I could sleep in the mornings because I taught piano starting in late afternoon, so I volunteered to do the night shift. When he died, I had been with him the night before and came home about 8:00 in the morning. Instead of going to bed I stayed up to do laundry. We lived in a split level house and from the lower level where the washer and dryer were I could look up a short flight of stairs into the kitchen. About ten o'clock that morning I looked up and there was my brother-in-law standing by the table in the kitchen wearing his fireman's uniform. He was a volunteer fireman when he became ill. He seemed to be thanking me for staying with him and telling me good-by. Incidentally, he was buried in his fireman's uniform. I had not told anyone about seeing him in it, except my husband, so had nothing to do with him wearing it to be buried.

Shortly after the funeral, feeling the need to get away, we went on a short weekend trip in our van. I could feel the presence of his brother in the van between us. I just knew he was there. I also had known he was at his own funeral. I could just feel it. The trip was probably about two weeks after the funeral.

Not long after this I had an out-of-body experience. Let me back up a moment and say that all through my life I would periodically get a "zing" that went through my head. It's hard to describe; it was sort of like a buzz but at the same time like an electrical shock. This would happen a lot if I would try to take a nap in the middle of the day, but it also happened when dropping off to sleep at night. I talked with my sisters about this and both they and my mother would get the same thing. Also, if I took a nap in the middle of the day and the sun was shining brightly I would sometimes wake up, but my body wouldn't. This also happened with my sisters. We would mentally jerk and try to wake up the body. One day I jerked and jerked, mentally, and couldn't wake my body up. The next time I jerked I found myself floating down the short flight of stairs and looking back up at my body lying on the bed. I seemed to be normal except for not having any feet. I just came to a point and floated instead of walking. I went on out into the kitchen and got a drink of water – mentally, of course, and the next thing I knew I was back in the body on the bed. It all seemed so very real. It was not like a dream. It was much more real than that; it was as real as anything I did in real life.

This incident started me searching for an answer as to what had happened to me. I wondered if I had died momentarily or just what did happen. I started reading Edgar Cayce books and Ruth Montgomery books. These were the only ones I could find on the subject at our small town library and I didn't want to ask anyone.

I told my husband about it and he said it was just a dream. He really didn't believe anything that happened to me – even about seeing his brother. I eventually dropped my searching, mostly because of my husband's attitude and the fact that about this time I discovered I was pregnant. What a shock that was after twenty years of not being able to have children.

Due to the illness of my brother-in-law and my staying at the hospital at night, my husband and I had not been sleeping together. Soon after the funeral we went on the short camping trip to New England. We were exhausted from the strain of the funeral and the camper did not lend itself to romantic situations, so we still hadn't "slept" together in the conjugal sense until the night the first men landed on the moon. It was pouring down rain in New England and we wanted to watch the moon landing on television, so we gave up camping for one night and rented a motel room. We didn't have much money so we put the room on our credit card. The bill for that room never came in and for some reason – I don't remember the exact circumstances – after we were home we couldn't locate an address for the motel so never paid for the room. That was the night our son was conceived.

All the time I carried my son I could feel his presence near me, especially when I would lay down to rest. I just knew that someone was with me. Of course I didn't know it was a boy at the time. The day he was born we had landed astronauts on the moon once again. We named him Neil Edwin after Neil Armstrong and Edwin Aldrich.

When Neil was about four years old, we rented out our home in Ohio and moved to Vail, Colorado. We lived in the ski town of Vail for approximately eighteen months. Nothing much took place in Vail as far as psychic experiences.

We left Vail and returned to Ohio for approximately two years. We then returned to Colorado, to the city of Grand Junction. Once we settled in Grand Junction I became very busy. Many events of a psychic nature took place. I had hurt my back helping my husband move a tent camper and while teaching at the music store that evening I knew I had to get some help for it. A coworker told me about his chiropractor. I had been to one once as a child when my neck was out of place and I was kind of scared of them, but took the number and made an appointment.

After having a series of adjustments I began having strange experiences in his office. After leaving the office there were times when I couldn't remember which end of the table my head had been at. Unbeknownst to me, the manipulations were opening my chakras.

My Path of Progress

From early adulthood on I remember having a strong conviction that communication between those of us on earth and those who had passed on was possible. I never did much about it only to read articles on the subject when I came across one. I also periodically would think "I wonder when my life is really going to start." This went on for quite awhile. Several years after I started channeling I was given the following explanation of what I chose to do this lifetime as far as goals, and how I reviewed the stages of the path.

From the Teachers and Guides

You, Norma, had achieved the bonding of the two halves of your soul in early lifetimes, but chose as your mission this time to review all stages of the path in order to teach it thoroughly to humanity so all would understand. You also chose to do it through the arts by bringing the Science of Music to the earth plane.

As far as reviewing, let us take my own case. I contacted a high level of the astral plane when I made my first breakthrough in channeling. These were the descriptions of the seven virtues I received the first day.

Let me back up a moment and say that unknown to me, I had previously been rising into the ethereal plane as far as writing the music and hearing it at night. This was inner plane, esoteric, activity. As far as exoteric contact – that made while immersed in daily life activity – I could not do that then as none can. All must work through the astral to be able reach the etheric in exoteric contact.

When I reached my twin reflection on the third level, I started receiving bad information. Some of it I even burned. This was all the bad traits that my twin was holding because the good traits were with me in incarnation. I took all the good with me into incarnation because I was determined to make spiritual progress this time.

After this stage of contact I still had to deal with the lower levels of plane three. I did not have to pass through planes one and two because I had entered above the sixth level of plane three. There is this dividing line. The lower levels of plane three are when the evil started coming through the writing. I remember one in particular that wrote "I am Dr. X and killed you in our previous life together." My twin tried to counteract these lower entities with true information, such as the fact that Dr. X and I had nine lifetimes together previously. Anyway this was a bad time for me as it is for all who persevere. (This is the point where my sister gave up when an evil low third plane entity threw her pencil across the room. This frightened her and she gave up.)

I entered at level nine at the left side of the brain, just ready to take the first step into the fourth section of the brain, the Spiritual Kingdom. I am a blend between the reasoning, intelligent mind's understanding of what is happening and the bare beginnings of spiritual essence. This is my place today in the scheme of things. This was my plan. This is what I'm working on now – the blending back over into the right side. In my next lifetime I will enter as a totally spiritual being, if I choose to come back

I am fulfilling my goals albeit slowly, but this is necessary. If I were to soar way out beyond most of humanity I would quickly lose them and not be able to achieve my goal of intelligently explaining the path of progress to others.

My Review of the Stages of the Path

Having begun music lessons and first grade at the age of four, my channel has been opening slowly from that time on. If what is known today of the whole process had been known then, I could have accomplished much more than I have so far in this life. The first display of the opening of the channel was in composing music. As mentioned previously, I had never tried to compose and on my fiftieth birthday I gave myself a present of devoting the day to trying to compose a song. I wrote four complete songs, words and music, some with many verses, that first day. I didn't realize this was unusual at the time. As I continued each day, the music literally poured out of me in almost perfect form. I would sit on the couch watching TV and writing music and wouldn't even listen to it until the next morning.

I decided to take a course in composition in the continuing education division of our local college to find out how to market the songs. Here I found out that composing doesn't usually happen this way. Most people work much longer, perhaps even a year or more on one song. By this time I was well on my way to writing the first of two musical plays. Looking back later, I realized that my compositions followed a growth pattern that matched my physical progress in music from the time of childhood. For instance, I started writing simple folk songs, (bluegrass music), then progressed through country, ragtime, big band, musical theater, religious, semi-classical and eventually country rock.

About the same time that I started to write music, I heard a beautiful chord from the music studio in my home. I was the only one at home and I could find no logical explanation. This caused me to resume my search into metaphysics which I had put on the "back burner" since having an out-of-body experience about twenty years before (I had learned that this was what happened to me when I left my body on the bed and went to the kitchen for a drink of water.) I joined a class at a local metaphysical bookstore in Grand Junction.

All through my review of the path there have been instances of clairvoyance and clairaudience. I'm going to relate some of them but I'm not going to try to arrange these in order because I can't remember the exact order they occurred.

- Soon after starting these classes I felt like there was a wire through the center of my body that was being pulled tighter all the time – similar to tuning a guitar string.
- One day while in the supermarket shopping, I was standing by the meat counter trying to decide which piece of meat to buy when I suddenly felt a force field around me, a large force field and very strong. I heard the words, "You belong to Him now. This is the way it happens." This was the only time I ever actually heard a voice. I finished my shopping quickly. The force field stayed with me even at the checkout counter. The checker and bag boy couldn't do enough for me. I've never received such prompt and courteous service anywhere either before or since, so I know that they felt something also. I went home and sat in a chair

98

for about two hours, almost in a daze, trying to figure out what was happening to me.

- No long after that experience, I was coming home from class one night when I saw flames running up a telephone pole that was near a building. As soon as I got home I called the fire department and reported it, but realized later that it something that only I could see.

- At one point, when Jesus-Sananda was coming through very strong I had the stigmata on my wrists and hands. There were four reddish spots or blotches, one on each hand and one on each wrist. This stayed with me for approximately three weeks. I never told anyone and would cover my arms and hide my hands so no one would see this.

- Another experience took place while a member of my seedcore was visiting from Canada. We were sitting in the living room along with my husband, when suddenly I jumped up and said, "An airplane just went down in the canyon behind our house. I was the only one who could see out the window which was behind the TV set we were watching. I ran outside and the others followed me. We could see nothing, but I called the local television station to report it. Needless to say, there was no plane; I was the only one who saw anything. I later asked my guides what they could tell me about the bright light with the tail that I saw outside my window Sunday evening that looked like it went down into the river canyon back of the house. I received the following answer: The light you saw was indeed seen with your third eye, which is opening wider slowly. This has been taking place for the last several months. These lights are all around you at all times. The ability to see them rests not only with the entity on the earth plane, but with us and our closeness to the earth plane and our desire to transvaporize our being. That was not a space ship; it was an actual entity of very high stature on the inner planes. He is approaching the orbit of your aura. This may seem like a strange way to phrase it but we will try to explain. A Master of high repute has become very interested in your work on the earth plane and is testing and trying the vibratory field, not only of your individual aura, but also of the aura of those around you and the aura of the geographical location on the earth plane. We do not know at this time what will be the outcome of his tests and his interest in you and your work. We can only wait and see as can you. Just continue as you have been. He will contact you when it is apparent he wishes to. The one, Donoray who was in your home twice in the past is part of the testing because he is of a lower vibratory field than this new Master. If this new Master desires to take you on as his chela (student), it will not be as his vehicle through which to speak, it will be as a Master teacher in the flesh that he will train you, as one who has earned the right to have the wisdom of the universes.

- Another time I was seated in the same chair watching TV and just at the stage of falling

Journeys in the Present

asleep when I saw a small figure, about four foot tall, dressed in black with gold braid and buttons like a uniform. It was off to the side of the TV between it and the fireplace. I asked about this later and was told it was Donoray.

- Later, when on my way to Canada to give a lecture-concert on The Science of Music, which a member of my seedcore had arranged, my husband and I checked into a motel room the night before we got to the city where the lecture was held. There quite often is a Bible in the room but this Bible was open on the night stand and as I leaned over to read the passage it was opened to I almost freaked out. It was a passage addressed to the "Master Musician."

- Yet another incident that took place was as follows: The girl who sang in my dance band was visiting in town one day and had come to see me and asked if she could stay there until time for an event she was to attend that night. I told her yes, but that I had to do some channeling and asked her not to disturb me while I was doing that. I closed the bedroom door and began. It wasn't long until I heard a knock on the door. When I opened the door she said, "There's something in your living room. I asked who it was and if they wanted to see me. She said, "No there's something in your living room. Come and see." As we went down the hallway and came to the living room I began to feel a very powerful force field – so powerful that I thought we were going to be electrocuted. It felt like a field of electric, effervescent bubbles. I was scared and

101

so was she. The hair was standing up on her arms. She said she had been washing up a few of the dishes with her back to the living room when she felt like someone was watching her. We almost ran out the front door. I didn't know what to do. I was going to go get my neighbor, but we decided to try to go back in. When we opened the door we could tell the field was dissipating. We stayed out a while longer and then went back in. This singer was not into metaphysics at all and was almost scared out of her mind. This incident was in the corner of the room where I would sit in the chair and channel, the same chair I would watch TV in and where I was sitting when I saw the plane and the figure dressed in black. In almost every instance the visual sightings were in the area of a television set – these later sightings that is, not the sightings I had twenty years or so before that.

- Also about this time I began to see what seemed to be the atomic make-up of different material. It was like I could look right through it and see the atomic structure of it.

- One other incident was while playing for church one Sunday, there was a beautiful vase of blue flowers near the organ. When I looked up at them the next time they were all outlined in red. It was the most beautiful sight I had ever seen. I'd never seen this before and haven't seen it since.

- I went to Fort Collins, CO to do a concert-lecture in the music recital hall. I would talk and then play one of my own compositions, then talk and then play. This lasted about an hour. Afterwards I had about five people come up to me and say they could see a huge figure overshadowing me – about twelve feet tall.

- Not long after this, at Christmas time, I was at the mall shopping and every child I passed looked at me and gave a great, big happy grin. This was very unusual because I had never made a fuss over kids. For the most part I would just ignore them unless they were a piano student. I had never done any baby-sitting as a teenager nor had I watched my nieces and nephews much. These reactions from the children seemed very unusual. Then, while still at the mall that evening, I met a woman who was in my metaphysical class. This particular woman could see auras. She spoke to me and then I saw her face change into a look of shock and disbelief. She muttered something like, "I've got to go," as she literally backed away from me looking very scared. She almost ran to get away. I don't know what she saw. She never told me.

- We studied the Alice Bailey books in the metaphysical class I attended and while studying at home I would sit with a paper and pencil to outline the chapter we were studying. I became very frustrated because I was much older than the rest of the class and wasn't as quick to understand. In fact I couldn't understand most of it. I was studying one day, outlining a chapter and trying to understand the difference between two words, indifference and impersonality, when suddenly I felt like the right side of my brain was stretching upwards. A beautiful childlike description of both terms came flowing in and, as I had paper and pencil right there, I wrote it down. We were studying a series of seven virtues so I decided to see if I could get descriptions of the rest of them. I did. This was the stage of my spiritual growth then. Now, ten years later, I'm writing about atoms and nuclear energy. What a fast rate of growth I've been on. Each day after that I rewrote the Alice Bailey book into simple language that I could understand. Then I began asking questions, not only about the book, but I realized that I could ask personal questions too. This was when I got into trouble because, unbeknownst to me at that time, when you first start to channel you reach the highest level of the astral plane first and work your way backward to the lower levels before breaking out into the clear transmissions of the forth dimension. So to start with the material was good but I went through a stage of being told some things by the lower evolved entities that weren't true. It was always in the realm of personal information that I was led astray by these lower beings. I finally worked through that stage and want to warn others that they will also need to work through it and continue reaching for higher material.

- The energy drain of channeling is one that is enormous for the human body. When I first began channeling, I would write by hand with a pencil, not a pen, and could only write less than a half page a day. If I overused the channel I would notice the energy loss in my speaking voice. (This is still true today.) I eventually built up my energy to where I could write six or seven pages a day with no ill effects. At one point, an entity played one of the piano compositions through me at a church service I was playing for. I started shaking and became sick in my stomach. I lost my voice for two weeks following that. I tried to channel on an electric typewriter, but the vibration of the typewriter made me sick in the stomach. I also tried talking into a tape recorder. This worked better, but was very slow at first. Then I would have to type the recorded work on the typewriter which I found very time consuming. About this time I learned to use a computer and found that I could type the channeled material directly into the computer without becoming ill and did not have to retype the material. Also I could correct typing errors quite easily. This became my preferred method of channeling. I can do vocal channeling, but was always quite timid and very self-conscious about doing it. Also, I always felt that I received more accurate information when I wrote instead of talked. I don't know if this is true or not. I don't think it is necessarily, but because talking was harder for me I had to focus more attention on it and couldn't get as deep into the material as I can when doing it on the computer. Now the channeling comes through when I'm talking as myself and most of the time I don't even realize it. (Is this the meaning of the Biblical saying, "My Father and I are one?")

- One night I woke up in the middle of the night and tried to open my eyes. The light was so bright it hurt them. Every time I tried to open them, the light would penetrate like a flash. I finally managed to get them open and the light coming in the window sparkled like diamonds, similar to the sun on snow, but much brighter and in a little larger flakes or diamonds. Between me and the window, not in a perfectly straight line, but a little to my right and about five foot off the floor was a dark blue (perhaps somewhat greenish also), transparent bubble about as big around as two foot in diameter. There was a thin rod protruding from it. The bubble seemed almost unimportant in comparison to the light coming in the window; not light streaming in, just filling the opening of the window perhaps, like it was outside. As I watched it faded in brilliance and the bubble disappeared. I closed my eyes and reopened them. The light was very dim, but still there and then faded entirely. I was a little scared, but more fascinated. One part of me seemed to tell the other I was scared, but the other part said there was nothing to be scared of. I went back to sleep with no problem. The following morning I felt very clear headed and as though my whole body had been energized. I asked my guides if I had seen them the previous night and also if they would explain the light. I received an explanation as follows: "Yes, you did see us. Nothing was any different from what we have been doing for almost three years, except that we woke you purposely so you could see and believe in the true sight of a UFO. It is time that all know of us. The light was the light from our larger craft outside and up in the air. The flashes you saw were made as the craft was leaving. The sparkles in the window that faded were from the crystalline energy left behind. Krystos energy is used for channeling from the higher realms. Normal ESP rides on the positive energy waves that spread out and disperse – become blurry at the edges. The Krystos energy curls in on itself and is a more pure form of communication. It was the beautiful crystalline energy you saw through your window with your third eye. The bubble was filled with information; the stick was the antenna. We were not in the bubble. It disintegrated in your bedroom as soon as the information in it had been transferred into your higher consciousness. It is these 'bubbles' that can float through any obstacle that contain the thoughts we want to pass on for the books. These bubbles are of a thin filament that, like a snag in a sweater, unwinds itself as it disseminates the information. It happens at an extremely fast rate of speed, so seems to disappear instantly. We can and will appear bodily to you soon, but you needed to have this first manifestation to prepare you. Please do not be frightened. It will seem to hurt your eyes, but in truth it will not, cannot hurt them; only can it help them." Since this time my distance vision had improved remarkably on my last two eye examinations and I now no longer need to have a prescription for distance.

Experiences Changed Me

All of these experiences have left me a totally different person. My goal is to get the teachings that I've been given out to the public in the best way that I can. I believe that some of the most important help for people would be in realizing that there is a structured path to opening up to the higher dimensions. I would like to outline that path for them by using my own experiences.

The first point of contact a person needs to make should be with the half of your soul that stayed on the inner planes to guide the half that incarnated. I jumped over this part and had to achieve this at a later date. When I started making contact, it was with the parts of me that I chose to bring into incarnation with me for their experiences and strengths. These were Francois, at dimension or level four, Charles, at level five and Philippe, at level six.

I was told later that Francois (Francois Couperin the musician contacted on the fourth dimension) is a student of Nicodemus (contacted on the ninth dimension, who had a previous incarnation as Tchaikovsky the musician). I was also told that Charles (the scientist contacted on the fifth dimension) is a student of Sashuyon (a scientist contacted on the tenth dimension.) They are all on the stream of consciousness that my seedcore has, as a stem up to the next higher field of the Oversoul. There are more, of course, and also I can follow branches of this main stream to connect to different beams or them to me. It is a fantastic network of communication lines. I was told to consider those on my stem to be local calls, the others, long distance

108

calls. The long distance calls cost more in energy than do the local calls.

When I got to level seven I started tapping into my seedcore which was Korlon and Kortina. Korlon is about three grades below Kortina, but they are both parts of my seedcore.

To explain a seedcore – as you keep coming back each lifetime you take the knowledge, understanding perhaps is a better word, that you have learned and mesh it with the previous incarnations through the seed core. The good is kept stored in this seedcore. The other is what is brought back into incarnation to be worked on, re-learned and re-experienced, because it wasn't acceptable to the standards of the seedcore.

Perhaps you come out of the incarnation with some concepts that were not acceptable. One of the concepts that I came out of the last incarnation with was that if you were multi-talented, if you had all the talent in the world and were able to do everything you wanted, painting, singing and all the different instruments and writing and everything, that you would be so popular you would have all the friends in the world. This was the concept that I came out of the last life with.

I had been a cleaning lady in a theater that lifetime and had stood in the shadows watching the performers on stage. It seems that I had been very lonesome in that last lifetime. I came out of that lifetime feeling that this was what I wanted the next time – to be a musician, an actor, an artist, an author, a dancer, etc. I came to the conclusion that the way to be popular, to be happy, to be rich, to have everything, was to have all this talent. This is what I took back from the last incarnation and presented to the panel of my seedcore that helped me evaluate that lifetime. They decided that this would form the basis of my next incarnation (my present lifetime in which I am multi-talented. I play and teach six different musical instruments, compose music, do oil painting, dance, give lectures, write musical plays and books, do web pages and design technological projects). It seems I had a lot of talent from previous incarnations of those in my seedcore to draw on. At the same time they also helped me set a spiritual goal that I would help humanity if I came back with all this talent.

At the end of this incarnation, I will form my own conclusions as to whether this theory was good or bad. Then I will take whatever my decision is and present it back to the seedcore to be accepted or rejected. This is the process we all go through.

For the whole first part of this life I had been reviewing and did not start my mission perhaps as soon as I planned and am feeling under pressure now to do a catch-up type of thing because it's all flooding in at one time. It should have been coming in at a slower pace from an earlier age on but I did not touch into the center of my being until my 50th birthday.

CHAPTER 7

A REVIEW

"I like this picture you drew of planet earth to use for the Science of Music Logo," I said to Neil as we continued going through the pictures on my computer.

Neil's Drawing of Planet Earth for Music Logo

"Was it difficult to draw?" I asked.
"No actually it wasn't – it was really kind of fun. The hard part was getting the music notes to wrap around the earth," Neil replied.
"You know, the TimeTraveler says we need to think of the earth as a space ship or a space station," I said.
"That is something that I have trouble doing," he replied. "I just can't seem to think of it that way."
"I have trouble with that too. Let's see what else the TimeTraveler has to say about it. Maybe it will help us in trying to picture it that way," I responded.

"Okay by me – maybe it will help," Neil said.

To Recap

To try and explain more fully, please picture the large physical bodies of the planets you see in the sky, as space ships or rather space stations, as that is what they are, even our home station earth. There are no true universes in our particular solar system, none that are manifested eternally in time and space. They are all satellites, if you will, or "space stations" or "space ships." Each one is a base for one of the spirit sons in the intermediate universe – pieces of the Creator's mind that broke off at the time of the "big bang."

The fountain that is inside everyone, the "rings of energy," the planets in our solar system, all have something different to offer each one that contacts them. There will be 12 levels of each planet (plane) on that beam of Holy Spirit inside you. Your ability to tap in is in direct relationship to your standing in evolution and your willingness to work on your attitudes and your willingness to search for answers from a deeper part of yourself than just the concrete mind, the animal brain, if you will. Humans certainly have far more available to them than they are taking advantage of.

The Process of Channeling is your Spiritual Journey

After working through the astral plane, the process of channeling, which is our esoteric or spiritual journey, works its way up through twelve dimensions. It does this hand in hand with our exoteric, physical growth through the twelve dimensions of the brain. As given before, there is no contact available with the first two levels or dimensions as they have been closed off to humanity. Therefore, after skipping levels one and two and working through level three and then the astral plane, our first breakthrough into the second mind section, the lower right side of the brain, is made. This is where true esoteric contact begins. What has come before this has been psychic phenomena contact.

Your guide (twin soul) and you quickly progress through all levels on planet five and become thoroughly familiar with all the implications of being whole again. It is at this point that your soul and personality begin working together. After this contact is made most people stop their progress. They are happy with themselves and their relationship with others and feel that they have reached a goal. The contact with plane five through your guide (reaching your twin) has such a beautiful, complete, whole feeling that most feel content and live out that incarnation with no more struggles or growth and no further steps on the ladder of evolution. (This would be the Biblical "heaven.")

Those who do go on are usually put under pressure to do so by their united seed-core, their teacher, who makes them aware of goals set before entry. You see, the two of you planned the progress for that incarnation and then, perhaps due to weakness in either half of the seed-core, neither progresses any further until the next incarnation. But if both halves of the divine spark are strong, then more progress will come.

Contact is continued to planet six where you, as a whole spark, plan the next stage of lessons and things you want to accomplish, (perhaps you decide you want to return to college or something, to relate this to earth plane life). As you continue and move on to planet seven, you realize you need to do something to help others.

The pattern world for earth is one of the higher planets, or should I say, earth is a copy of and a satellite station for a higher planet. The only way they have of contacting those on earth is by transmissions such as I am engaged in or by coming down in their smaller ships from their mother ship or satellite or space station.

To review, the first contact humanity has is with the astral plane which is above our planet, extending for miles between our manifested plane and the ethereal body of our planet, which is above the astral plane. You have the ability to contact those above you on the earth's twelve planes ascending, either with a physical plane teacher, or an inner plane guide if no physical teacher is available.

When you have reached beyond the twelfth plane of the earth's ascending twelve planes, your continued contact is with the twelve levels of the astral plane starting with the twelfth. You work your way up through those twelve levels, which are backwards. Therefore, the higher you go, the less evolved the contacts you make and this is the really dangerous period for all humanity. This is the area that scares most people off. This is the area that frightens the churches. This is a problem.

Humanity needs to be educated about this area, warned of it, and therefore by being made aware they can, by using their intelligent mind, make sure they do not get caught on this plane by devious manipulating souls who are waiting there and studying before reentering manifestation.

Now, whatever level of advancement you are working on (most are on level three or perhaps some are on four) you can safely be in contact with this pole, the beam inside you as follows: We will use a person of level four advancement as an example.

They can contact level:

5
6
7
8
9
10
11
12 of the earth plane

Then they reach level:

12 of the astral plane
11
10
9
8
7
6
5
4

A person can even contact level four and still be safe, although you will not learn anything more than you already know. Levels one and two are not permitted much freedom, so will not be much of a problem. Therefore, your main danger area lies in the third level of the astral plane, the inner plane. Here you will find relatives and friends who were at this level when incarnated on the earth plane and they will try to cling to you and hold you there. Also, here you will find religious fanatics who will press their views on you of the crucified Christ that was the extent of their progress on earth. When you finally break free of this zone, you reach those on level one of the fourth dimension on up to twelve and then on up to planet (plane) five, levels one through twelve; then planets 6-7-8-9-10-11 and 12. Twelve levels of each. Level twelve is where the entity giving this material just was. This entity is now on level one of the ethereal body of twelve. After many more years of teaching from here, he will move on to the next solar system.

The rings of energy start at level one, planet four. Anything you reach up to that point was not from a ring of energy. It was from levels on a pole of energy.

Your Third Eye Is Your Power Converter

Yes, those contacting me (Norma) are in space ships coming from their mother ship and trying to reach into the higher minds of individuals. This is why we see them with our higher mind through our third eye. Our third eye is our "power converter," so to speak. It converts their energy into our dimension, so that they may be seen. They are the ones that can give the best guidance to our "guide," our twin, our higher mind.

The space ships we see with our own eyes are not from our solar system and will not give help that is going to help the individual. They are of a lower vibration, those we can see without using our "power converter." They are not dangerous or mean or to be feared, they just are not able to contact us through our inner being to be able to guide us that way. They can give information that is startling and scary and this information can lead to science fiction movies and books and in that way they are workers of the light helping with the awareness plans, but they are completely unable to help humanity find the God Within themselves.

There is nothing wrong with contacting them except the danger of not moving past them into those of our own solar system. They are to be found around all planets in our solar system and some of them are from very advanced worlds, but those worlds are too far ahead of us to give those of us on the earth plane any help for our inner journey. The only danger in transmission from them is that it doesn't lead us to inner growth spiritually. Because they can be seen with the concrete mind, they are much more believable and people want to contact them, because they can see them. This doesn't take as much work on raising our own consciousness as does the contact with our own solar system, our inner universe.

Those staying in touch with space ships we see with our own eyes are shortchanging their inner growth. This is the easiest contact and the first contact made by a beginning psychic and it's okay for a while, but we must move on and go inward to contact those who can help us find our Godhead, the apex of our mind where we will find our God Within. When this has been accomplished, then contact with those in space ships from outer space will be more meaningful and understandable to humanity.

To explain inner and outer spacemen, the inner are the guides and teachers that inhabit any of the planets in our solar system. Their duties are to help those on our planet understand their heritage as far as the lesson plan for our solar system. This includes finding the God Within ourselves that must be found before progress can go past the earth plane. There are several things inside our mind that need to be located and understood and used at the start of our inner journey, which is what the spiritual journey is, an inner journey.

Rings of Energy are Ever Present

The circles of light, the rings of energy, are ever present. Our ability to reach them depends on our desire to reach them and the desire we have for spiritual fulfillment and for the wisdom and knowledge of our great universe. If the desire is not there, the flow of knowledge will not be started because desire is what primes the pump to start the flow. If this is dwindling we have only ourselves to look to for the answer of why it is dwindling. If we do not take the time to digest and synthesize what we have already received – which will then, in turn, bring forth more desire for further knowledge or clarification – then the flow decreases. Those in the higher planes are not allowed to contact us or "bug" us, if you will, to give us information. That is a function of the lower planes. When contacting the higher planes we are more truly than before directing the energies. On the lower planes they will direct us or try to. When we progress to the higher planes we must see our path and plan that path and direct the help we can receive into the field of interest that we have.

From the Teachers and Guides

We would like to explain the relationship between Norma and Master and Donoray and the new group, etc., in terms relating to your system of schooling to help with understanding.

- Kindergarten - We would place Norma in "kindergarten" at the beginning of her life. She moved through stages of review as a child until reaching the "ninth grade," which was the grade she left off in the last life. (Norma has been told several times previously that she entered on the 12th life of the ninth level or mind dimension.) (Incidentally, Norma went through an exoteric move at the beginning of the ninth grade in real life.) When reaching this point she began her inward journey that went back and started kindergarten over again as a review on the inner planes with kindergarten being the time needed to become acclimated to esoteric review and three school grades for each of the three entities, Francois, Charles and Phillipe.
- Grades 1-2-3 - Francois
- Grades 4-5-6 - Charles
- Grades 7-8-9 – Phillipe - This brought the esoteric part of her up to level nine. While doing this she branched out to make contact with the central pole of knowledge surrounding the earth plane. This allowed her contact with teachers and guides. Christ Michael was at level twelve of this stationary pole of knowledge. At the same time that Norma continued contact with the stationary pole she was reaching grade ten and regained contact with pure

119

essences of her own beingness. This would be Tasha at grade nine.

• Grade 10 - Sashuyon and Donoray - When Norma reached "grade ten" – Sashuyon and Donoray – she reached the ability to do "outside research" with other scientists that are not on the faculty of her school. Nicola Tesla would be one of these.

• Grade 11 - Ezekiel - Ezekiel has left the earth plane and is located on the planet Nebudon.

• Grade 12 - Master - Master at grade twelve is comparable to Christ Michael at grade twelve, only Master is as an individual grade twelve and Christ Michael an overview grade twelve. She has since passed them both up, as far as channeling points, due to the nature of her mission. Everyone can reach Christ Michael – only Norma and her twin spark can reach Master and he will be the dual Master with Norma reaching one half of this Master and her twin spark reaching the other half of this Master. This will be true for all, but the masters are twins in the case of Norma and her twin.

• College - When she reached the group called "the others," she contacted those in "college" who had graduated from her own school. Those she contacted were as freshmen in college. She will progress through to the senior year of college, then back up and start with outside schools from freshman to senior.

• Graduate School - Her next ability will be to be able to contact graduates of other schools. Then she will go into "graduate schools," both her own alma mater and those of others. At that point she will start on the pure life of spirit. She may accomplish this before her earthly demise. If so, much more explanation of the wondrous workings of the universes will be able to be brought down to the earth plane. If she does not reach this level before her earthly demise she can choose to continue to give this to those on earth by accessing and sending this information through her twin spark (who will outlive her on the earth plane). It will still be the masculine and feminine energies cooperating; only the esoteric will truly be the esoteric part of her twin at that time. This gets quite difficult to understand and, as stated, the relationship between Norma and her twin should be charted and detailed and saved for humanity to understand their path.

Twin Sparks

The information about twins explains those who only channel one entity – this is the course they have followed. They chose to do this for the sake of humanity. In the case of Jane Roberts and Seth, both halves of the twin sparks are now on the inner planes. In the case of Jack Purcell and Lazarus, one is and one isn't. We could give more examples, but would always prefer to give material that deals more with the majority of the people rather than the minority, because we are trying to bring understanding to the masses.

You, Norma, are to serve as an example. Therefore, it will seem as though it is you, but know in your heart that you have all this help within you. You will never, ever walk out in front of a crowd or audience to speak or to play music alone – ever! And yes, you are to take the credit and the bows for it on that plane because this is the way humanity will accept it. It is becoming much easier for you and me to talk, as these are practice sessions and we're not delving into deep philosophical material at this time. We do not want to. We simply want to practice this way.

This is how your channel has been trained to work. At the present moment, yours is still in the rough stages. You are to be able to flip flop from you down there to us up here at any given time with no noticeable effort on your part. It is a mental process. We are in your mind. Think of it as a tiny door and see the door open when you want to access us. We suggest you try this with your tape recorder as practice. Ask yourself one question at the beginning of the practice that you, yourself, don't know the answer to or have any thoughts on. Start talking into the tape and see this little door open and let the answer come through. This is a very good way to practice. Incidentally, when channeling and you need to go deeper, just close your eyes and bow your head momentarily and you will go deeper. Breath deep and stand tall.

Energy Use in Channeling

When using the computer to give readings for others at a distance, I pick up their feelings and even their physical pain. A strange effect that I sometimes have is at times I feel lop-sided as though the computer keyboard is wavy or tipped or turned in an odd direction. In other words I either feel like I'm gliding up over a hill or that my head is turned at a different angle than it actually is. I didn't know if this is due to a physical condition in my body, such as a low energy level, or if it had to do with either the person I was doing the reading for, the geographical location of that person or the type of waves the material was being sent in on. I asked about this and the answer I received was:

You are lopsided at that moment because of the energy waves being pulled into the right side of the brain. They are heavy because of the force. Force adds weight to this type of wave length. This is something your scientists should think about. This is why you feel as though you are leaning top heavy or side heavy as it were. This is lower right brain activity. When you work with your charts, thinking them through or you're editing, it is upper left brain. At night when you sleep you spend most of your time in the upper right. You do not do much living in the lower left anymore and this is how it should be for more of humanity, or most of humanity at this time. There truly is nothing to worry about – in fact, this will become more noticeable. As you continue to teach and lecture you will find this happening. Know when it does that it is only because the energy is strong and pure and true and relax in this knowledge of drawing in perfect, strong energy for the sake of teaching humanity.

Anytime another wants to communicate with Norma, such as Tesla or Mafu, they must use the energy of Master and Donoray or, in other words, Norma's energy in the higher vibratory fields. We must give the permission because we are the only ones who know what this energy level is and what it is capable of handling. This is why they must have our permission. It would be an invasion of our privacy, and therefore Norma's privacy, if just anyone could come through. So even if they have the most valuable information to give, they still must have our permission first so there is never a danger to the channel. We are ever protective of her energy levels. The more energy she has the more freedom we have in granting permission. This allows her to do more channeling and also allows us to give more entities permission to give information; only accurate and highly evolved information and teachings will be allowed and when the focus must be on a certain area, the information must relate to that area.

Norma is Also a Channel on the Inner Planes

Norma had a dream at one point about someone channeling through her on the inner planes. This can happen. Norma, being a channel on the earth plane is also a channel on the inner planes. This talent crosses dimensions the same as all other talents such as playing piano or art, etc. The one who spoke through her was very powerful and she was aware of this. He used her etheric energy up the same as a powerful one coming through her on the earth plane will use her physical energy up.

The gist of his warning was that times are becoming so perilous on the earth plane that humanity needs to listen to what is coming through the esoteric channels if there is to be any hope to save them and the planet. Things are going awry so fast that it is frightening when even those from the outer planets come through with a warning. This is an indication that many hard times are ahead for humanity and without a serious turnabout on the earth plane there will be no way of stemming the tide of decay and demoralization that is approaching.

We only wish to give this information in amounts that can be understood by not only Norma, but all who read this. When it is presented to humanity it should not all be given in one dose. They will need to have time to adjust as each stage unfolds. Remember this please when preparing items for publication.

At times we are on our own planet, other times we are a cell in Norma's brain and yet other times we are a gamma ray. We would like to explain the relationship between these three statements, and how we can be in all three states or places at the same time. When we speak of being in the different places or in different states of being, it is because of the three different universes, the Macro, the Human and the Micro. We exist in all three at the same time. It is comparable to you having different facets expressing on different levels of reality. When expressing in the Macro Universe, the large universe, we are on our own planets. When expressing in the Human universe we are in Norma's brain cells and when expressing in the Micro universe we are gamma rays.

The reason it comes out in the material in different ways at different times depends on where we are when doing the dictating. We can dictate to Norma from any of the different universes. Remember, at one time we explained that the material is given and perhaps not recorded on the earth plane until a later date. Say, for instance, we dictate from our own planet and give material ahead. When Norma does the writing it comes out as though we are on the planet at the time it is being given. During the same session we may decide to give more. This will be when we enter the brain cells of Norma and the material will come from that area. The same is true when we are free roaming gamma rays. We may momentarily enter Norma's brain and dictate something that will not be written until later. She then receives it as though coming from a gamma ray. No matter which area it seems to come from, it all goes directly into her brain cells at the time it is dictated. It then depends on when it is retrieved by her as to how it relates as to where we are. We are here ever much nearer the surface now than at any time in the past. This is what we want you, Norma, to realize is that we are you. You are the one with this enormous storehouse of knowledge and can tap into it at your leisure. It no longer requires that you do certain rituals or anything. All you have to do is ask, even just mentally and then sit quiet for at least 30 seconds. Do not let your mind race off to another question before the first one is answered. This is what you do, you know.

My Personal Goal Related To Channeling

My personal goal is to enlighten others as to what to expect when channeling and to encourage them to keep moving and demanding more in-depth material, and not to get stuck on the astral plane. What I, and others before me, went through was not always pleasant; at times it even was frightening because we didn't know what was happening. For instance there comes a point when the energies are no longer allowed to come through and contact you. There is a turn-around and the energy starts to pull away causing you to reach higher and harder for contact. This is when the point comes that you must ask them for help; they cannot offer it to you and cannot step in unless you ask them. If one doesn't know this he would merely give up on channeling, thinking it was ended; it is not, it is merely a sign of progress. The more blended you become with the energy, the more progressed on the spiritual path you become. The true test of progress is always, of course, in the quality of material received and the manner in which it is presented to your fellow human beings. There will be no self-glorification in one who is in spiritual harmony with the higher dimensions.

The Guides' Goals in Channeling

Your first biggest step needs to come in the area of belief in not only yourself, but also in us. We are very real you know; we are not figments of your imagination. Also we need to state that you, Norma, are not a split personality, just one with many different shining facets that need to express. Let them each express in their turn when the time is right, but know that they are all you, a many faceted being. Please do not put up blockages against us or against any of the facets of your personality. You cannot repress them or us and have any growth. We will remove all blockages from your stepping forward at this time. We are not overstepping our boundaries when we give compensations, only if we remove needed lessons. What we are removing will be blockages that are preventing these lessons from being learned. We are not removing the lessons; we cannot remove the lessons, only make them more accessible. For instance, many people have problems of the personality that were mostly caused by early childhood upbringing. An example would be never learning how to accept and give love. This situation might have been chosen if an entity's mission is to bring the concept of earth plane love and relationship into focus for the seedcore. This is the way guidelines are brought into focus and the next issuance of that seedcore will use these guidelines for the next incarnation onto the earth plane.

There is so much that needs to be brought through that we need to have every available channel to be able to help humanity as things get tighter and tighter on the earth plane as far as vibratory rate. The changes are becoming closer as far as earth changes and devastation will hit most every part of the world in the next twenty years. So you can see how desperately we need to have good channels like yourself. There will be compensations in this lifetime for those who give of their time freely.

I, Donoray, am Norma as she will appear on the earth in the incarnation after the next in approximately three hundred years. At that time there will be another incarnation two lifetimes ahead that I will be in communication with to further this work on the earth plane. The next lifetime for Norma will be one for rest from technical duty and will allow much beautiful growth of her soul in which relationships will take a much more prominent part – relationships and the beauty side, the emotional side, of music which she has held in check in this lifetime to concentrate on the technical. Yes, indeed, lives are planned and laid out this far in advance when you reach a certain stage of evolution. No lifetime will be lived that does not have a specific purpose to be achieved. Lifetimes at a lower level of evolution will not be so focused. Thank you and good day.

CHAPTER 8

THE STEP UP IN MENTAL PROCESSES

"This is a pretty good picture your friend drew of a computer for me to use, isn't it?" I asked Neil as we continued looking through a file of clip art his friend had drawn for me to use.

"Yeah, he's a pretty good illustrator. I like his work," Neil replied.

"So do I and he doesn't want any credit given to him as the artist. The drawings are certainly very usable to illustrate different things in the notebooks," I answered.

"Why did you want a drawing of a computer?" Neil asked. "Did the Timetraveler compare a computer with something he was talking about?"

"As a matter of fact, he did," I replied. "He actually compared our brain to a computer. It's very interesting. Shall we tune in and find out about it?" I asked.

"Sure, let's do it," Neil answered.

Brain Compared to Computer

The goal for humans is not so much to become blended, although this does happen, as it is to insure that the computer can be accessed in all its many files. We would ask that you compare the brain with a computer that has the biggest hard drive available and multiply that by 1000. This will give you some idea of the holding capacity of the brain's computer. What happens in Alzheimer's disease is similar to a certain track on a certain disk becoming impaired for some reason, perhaps disuse, or even the crossing of some of the patterns at the time material was being stored. The ultimate goal for humanity is to have access to this computer at all times throughout all lives. This is a divine right of the human race and this is our goal.

From the Teachers and Guides

The addition of Donoray to the channeling group when Sashuyon needed to go on R & R (rest and restoration), was a step up in your mental processes as needed to continue to bring through technical aspects of the work. You had to make the decision to make this step. It could not be forced on you. When a step up is made this way there is no going back. As you continue to open the higher levels of the mind your dissatisfaction with the earth plane increases, thereby making a difference in your relationship with everyday life and the people you are involved with. You can stay at this level if you choose, if you are in harmony and balance with your exoteric life. By climbing higher and higher the exoteric life will be more difficult to balance. As the functions of the mind increase in vibration so also must exoteric situations and associations. Those who do not progress forward will begin to drag, so to speak, on your vibration. Therefore, those whom you associate with are very important. Donoray has always been in the upper levels of your mind. You have never reached for him until now. There are more at his level and higher that will come forward when invited.

Work Done on Channel at Night

Much work is done on the channel at night. One night I was seeing something that looked like two canoes or two hot dogs, as I called them then. I was told that they were a separation of the pineal gland. Thus far it had been whole. That night it was separated into two. Until then, only Tasha had permanent residence there. It seems I had invited Donoray in to also take up residence. I had a feeling of the left side of my body stretching larger. This was similar to my experience when I felt the right side of my brain stretch up. That was when Tasha entered. His entrance was not as full and all-encompassing as Donoray's was. Tasha grew after entry. Donoray entered full grown. That is evidently why I felt my whole left side stretch, not just my head. Donoray is on the left side because I invited him to partake in the exoteric affairs. Tasha is only involved with esoteric. Donoray is still at the tenth dimension the twelfth level, but due to the circumstances of his participation in my active life it was determined that he would take up residence in the left hemisphere, leaving the right for my inner path on this journey. At that time, Donoray and I would share the left side, Tasha and I the right side. All have access now to Master. Not just the right side, but also the left side of the brain can now reach Master.

From the Teachers and Guides

One other reason for this step is due to the vocal channeling. It must come through the exoteric part of you and with Donoray installed in the left side of the brain which controls conscious actions this will become easier. With him in the left brain, the access to the scientific material will be easier. As it was before, with him in the right, he had to access the left to reach the scientific. This way will work much better. This was a new stage in your channeling experience. We trust it was a pleasant experience for you. We knew that it would help the projects you were embarked on go more smoothly. It was a hard transition for you, but things have gone much easier since then.

Time to Finish Projects

I, Norma, expressed a "fear" or concern that there is so much involved in the Science of Music that I couldn't possibly live long enough to finish all that has been outlined. I received this answer:

This is in your control. The harder you work to bring this facet of your being into focus, the quicker all the many projects can come into manifestation. By using music and art and creative projects of beauty you will hold Donoray in existence in perfect partnership with you. It has been a long hard road. Now is the time to reap the rewards of your hard work, but this will take even more work on your part.

You must work to allow every part of you expressing on the earth plane to subjugate yourselves to Donoray. In other words you must "take a back seat" and let this beautiful, majestic facet of your being come to center stage, in this the central part of your earth plane existence.

"She" is a "he" also, but because of the body you are enclosed in Donoray will appear to those who are able to see her as a female. It matters not as the qualities of positive and negative are perfectly blended. You may choose to do this in two ways. You may totally become Donoray and "bury" Norma completely underneath this new facet or you may choose to share equally the earth plane existence, with Donoray and Norma being equal and one or you may go back and forth from one personality to the other. The true, proper, spiritual way, when one reaches this stage, is total blending into one composite being that allows the facet of Norma to live out her years in the planned manner and also serves her spiritual goals by allowing total expression of the beauty and talents and knowledge of Norma.

None else have had this decision to make. Not even the man Jesus reached this point. He had to bury the man Jesus and allow the facet expressing the Christ Consciousness full control of the latter part of the earth life. We do not wish for you to do this in this manner. We would like humanity to see the way it should be accomplished. For this reason you will be allotted enough years for this to take place. While you are allowing this process to happen, the material for all these projects will flow through and those who are in a position to bring them to manifestation will be drawn to you. This is a very rare happening on the earth plane today. You are a very special entity to have achieved this status. Be aware of this but do not let it color your actions. Donoray will guide and control the blending. You will continue on with the way you have been and your higher guidance will protect you while merging with you. You have been through a long session of channeling, first your past lives, and your present day guides and teachers and the universal mind. Now your channeling will be coming from your future lives, those whom you have given birth to through all your footsteps thus far as an expression of the Creator. May you be blessed my child. This is Christ Michael talking to you this morning. Peace be unto you.

Channeling Goes Better

The channeling went better after this. I felt very strong and different. There was a different feeling in my head, kind of like a connection that was pulling equally from both sides and holding things in balance. Before there had been a pulsing light on the right side only. This now seemed to be closer to the front of my head.

I was told that a given transmission will come through just one of the individuals in the master conglomerate and the teachings will be given as they relate to each one of these teachers individually. For instance messages coming from Mafu, one of the teachers from the eleventh dimension, always seemed to be from the angle of championing females – helping them find their power and use it. They said that it is a very natural thing to do and that this does happen often where one is representing the whole. They said that it would be the same as a spokesman for a company on the earth plane explaining the different projects from his point of view. If one person talks of a particular project it will be from a totally different angle than if another talks about it. They will all be talking of the same project and giving the same information and goals and concepts and theories, but each of them would come at it from their own understanding, which comes from their own backgrounds and places of activity within the project

.

One Main Channel or Stream

The next stage I reached was that of the chakras bonding into what would be one main channel or power stream. It needed to have the opening of the heart chakra which finally took place. This seemed to be my new transformed mind that was ready for much more brilliant ideas and wisdom and also was now able to accept and understand that which it was not ready to see before. This new brilliant mind is composed of all parts of me that are in transition to bonding all as one. The teachers told me:

Your guidance system is truly in place now. Listen to it. It helps you realize that no one can make you do anything that feels wrong for you. If it feels right, do it; if it feels wrong, don't do it. This goes for whatever suggestions are made for you by anyone. We, your other facets, are all with you at all times. We are here now and you will not lose any of the other connections such as your higher mind and your inner child, along with others of your conglomerate who have been with you helping and guiding until we could be brought into the picture. You have just added to them gloriously because we will magnify the voices that come from the other cells of your body. Until now, they have not been as clear and loud as they should have been. But now, there will be no mistaking what you know from all the cells in your body, your whole complete beingness. It is all integrated; just trust us that it is and that you are clean, clear and beautiful.

They always knew what I was thinking and they would gently chide me when they sensed my disbelief by saying things such as:

Why do you not have belief in us when we give things like this? We urge you to please be about altering the ego or doubt portion of your mind that comes from lack of trust which, then, is fear. No more depression. No more doubt. No more lack. No more fear. Just love of life which we know you can accept. It's that simple. You are the controller of your own destiny. We are here to magnify and further that destiny, but you are the creator of it. Be about creating what you want. It is true. The kingdom of heaven is now yours. The God Within you is complete and whole and powerful and beautiful.

As far as free will and independent study, none of this has been taken from you. We could not do that and would not do that. It is against universal law. But what happens, is this ability opens up such a vast area for independent study and the free will to do so, that you can pick any subject and become an expert on it. In your case, you have dedicated the ability and your life to trying to help humankind understand themselves. This was a choice made with your own free will and a subject to focus on that is the most fascinating and encompassing of all subjects available.

Contact with the Abraham Documentation Council

The next step up happened in the following manner. At one channeling session I, Norma, was told that:

We, your channeling group, includes Master and Abdo, also Tasha and Donoray. You will have one of us for each subject. Tasha will be for physical, Master for emotional, Donoray for mental, and Abdo for Spiritual. Abdo stands for Abraham Documentation. It is a different division of the Abraham Conglomerate than that which speaks through Esther Hicks. She is working with specifics; you are working with the overview which is just under the Creator God for spiritual subjects. The four areas of subject matter – physical, emotional, mental and spiritual – are in alignment from Abdo down from the top, just dropping enough to be able to tap into the different parts of the human makeup.

Part of those who communicated through you in the beginning are now part of the Abraham conglomerate as it comes through Esther while you have moved on to meet the requirements of your mission and taken a different turn of interest. Those who did not want to pursue what it is you want to pursue, joined our conglomerate. Your conglomerate is a very high order of world or global education. This is where your mission lies, all areas of education from the very youngest to the very wisest to the very oldest and to all nations but most particularly in the realm of the Science of Music as the new tool of education. It can progress much further than you have taken it thus far. It is time to rethink and update that information you received earlier. You have progressed all aspects of it much, much further than you could ever believe. Make contact with your inner guidance conglomerate which, of course, includes your higher self, who by the way is absolutely glorious, and continue to refine the Science of Music and apply it to all aspects of education on the earth.

You see, Abdo, himself, could not bring concepts down low enough to fit the human mind. His mental thought would be far too complex, his emotional body would not be understandable and there is absolutely no way he could begin to understand your physical body due to not ever having taken on one. This is why the teachers must descend to bring the teachings down. It has to be this way. But remember, Abraham is a huge teaching conglomerate and you are working with those at the top. All channeling on the earth at this time in your country is coming from this same pool. It is because of the origins of the human species and the infiltrating of spirit that was done in the beginning. This is too difficult to go into now. Other planets have their teaching conglomerates also. Occasionally some from earth tap into those, but the material that will help planet earth will be sent through this one conglomerate, the Abraham conglomerate, which is made up of many, many different sections. You are working with the top. We feel we must tell you this to give you the assurance you need to have faith and belief in what you bring through. The material we will send will end up being that which will ultimately turn the human race around and allow them to become divine beings. Please continue your mission. We love you. You must be flexible and shift with the tides.

Abdo and council is, as given previously, the Abraham Documentation Council which we prefer to call Abdo. It is of the highest sight and value for your earth planet. The level at which you reach us does not deal with material for the individual. This is left to others. This is not the domain of the Abdo Council. We can give "generalized information only" for humans, and will be glad to do so. We do not work in the area of personal growth. This is left to others. Our main thrust is on the understanding of environmental

138

changes, societal changes, educational changes and spiritual understanding. You are one of few channels that can reach some of this information and we desperately need to have your services to bring understanding and, with understanding, reconstruction of present practices in all areas. Thank you. We love you and receive you with open arms. All will work out for the publishing of the material with your determination and strength and willingness and love on the earth plane to put it into manifestation. Good day.

Vocal Channeling

Once, while getting ready to practice vocal channeling, I asked the following question: I would like to access the channel in the way that is most proper and necessary and fitting for me to do it, be it going through the movement of the neck that other channels use or not, I am very willing to do this if it will bring it through in the way that is necessary. I also would like to know by what name the channel should be called. You know how the people are. They want a name to attach to it and I would like some thoughts on that. Thank you and I am willing to go however deep you need to have me go in vocal channeling. If you need to have me to step aside totally and not recall anything that's done, I am willing to do that at this point. I understand this is not the way I've been taught to do it, but if this is what's necessary, I am willing. I don't want to practice long, but I would like to give this a try now. Thank you. The answer I received was:

Yes, we are here. Thank you. As you felt there was one motion. The dropping of the neck was all that was necessary in your case and will be from now on all you need to do. Drop the neck and then throw it back, not throw it, but just move it back and maybe once to each side. Everyone is different and this is all we need to come through to enter your body and we thank you for this opportunity.

Now as far as the question you asked, as far as a name, we would like you to just give it the name of Master. We could give it a fancy name; you could give it the name of whichever one of us is answering if you think that would be a good idea. You are the one on the earth plane who knows better than us. We are all your guides and all your teachers, your inner being. We are all of them and we are also able to tap the conglomerate in the high end of the conglomerate and when we do this, we would probably want it known that we are going out.

This is difficult to know exactly how to plan this. We will try this again. You are not the type of channel who will go away and not remember any of it. You basically are going to be directing most of it. Most of the questions will be answered from the part of you that you have known as Tasha. When it gets into the scientific realm, of course Donoray will be the one that comes through and when it gets into the spiritual questions, Master will be the one coming through. Tasha will take care of the physical and the emotional questions dealing with those parts of the human being. Donoray will deal with the mental/scientific and Master/Abdo with questions pertaining to the spiritual. It would depend on what level you need to go to as to which one it is in which case as far as the spiritual. It will start out as Master and ascend to Abdo.

We still think that putting the term Master on it, your Master teacher would cover all aspects because it is your entire channel. It is all your master teacher and the different aspects will address those questions which fall into their expertise. It is as simple as that and it can be explained as that. If they want to know the names, give them the names, but in the long run if you just simply say your Master teacher, we would prefer that. If they want an over-all name, probably Tasha would be one that would attract their attention. Donoray is a very strange name and Abdo is an abbreviation. Therefore, we really think Master would be the best.

At the moment you are talking to an advisor of Abdo who loves him very much and knows that he directs his conglomerate, his council with much love and devotion. You are the lowest member of his council. That is because you are on the earth plane and cannot raise your vibration up anywhere near his. He uses a group of seven to step his thoughts down to you. These seven are in addition to Tasha, Donoray and Master who are truly a part of your own seedcore. They are permanent residents in the lining of your brain. The others, Abdo and council are not permanent as yet. They will be when you are ready to assume your true mission. When you accept this responsibility then will Abdo become you.

Abdo and his wise council of seven will, at that time, use your body to speak through at all times when you are in association with those who would be your students. You are thinking you do not like what we are saying. You have not wanted to see the truth from the beginning of this. This is why it is you, the very reason that you have been chosen is because you do not want to be. Do you understand what we are saying?

To be the one chosen to bring the true spiritual teachings onto the earth plane does not mean that you have to give up your personality. On the contrary, it means that we want you to let the higher beings express through this beautiful personality at all times. Do not deny us as part of your beingness. Do not be embarrassed. You have worked hard and you deserve all the good things that are coming your way.

Now to get back to the problem at hand. Your personality still mixes with the lower end of your personal channeling group. Instead of the channeling group influencing your personality, it is still not quite balanced in that your personality influences your lowest part of the channel. Therefore, we do not want you doing personal readings, as given before, because this allows this improper influencing to take place. We want you to only access Donoray or higher. The beings that need to give more specific advice on the solar will have to be accessed through Donoray and their information will be passed on to you. Your channel is strong enough to do this without any coloration of the material.

Now you are thinking that if Tasha is the other part of your soul on the inner planes and you are not allowed to access him, that this does not seem right. It works like this. Tasha will be incorporated into the Donoray and Master figures. This is a matter of spiritual growth. It is part of the integration of the three parts of the physical body which must take place before spirit, Abdo, can have full expression. Therefore, from this time on, your other half of the soul on the inner planes is no longer located in your emotional body but is, instead, part of your mental body and is slowly going to be integrated into your spiritual which is the one you call Master. Your see, you have a spiritual body which is part of the physical body and then you have spirit itself which is not part of the spiritual body until total systhesization has taken place. This gets quite complicated and we will pursue it further at some other time as you are becoming confused. Study this much and ask again about it. For the time being know that you will be accessing Donoray and Master in conjunction with Tasha and always ask for an end assessment from Abdo.

Contact with Jonathan

The first mention of an entity called Jonathan was as follows: Sometimes the material comes partly from Tesla and partly from one who is working with us on a level slightly below our level which is the twelfth level. They are not in the habit of signing their names. This would be if Donoray was not able to be with you. This does not happen often, but occasionally he must take care of his own spiritual progress. He was coming up for a move onward and upward onto the eleventh level. He will still be able to be with Norma on all the projects but will occasionally have to call on help from others because he will be taking on additional duties. He is still in charge of all the projects. They will be finished to the point where he can leave them when it is necessary for him to leave them.

There are many studying under Tesla on this side, as his helpers. The one who worked with Tesla yesterday has been with him the longest. He will soon be moving up and will become more and more available. His name is Jonathan.

I believe Jonathan is a higher aspect of Donoray, who moved up in progress. The following came through several years later after the projects had been stopped for a while:

Yes, I am Jonathan. I am with you as always. I guide silently through the thought processes for the most part. When you drop below level ten you cannot reach Jonathan.

You must stay at level ten, the reasoning, wondering, questioning mind, in order to receive directly from him. If you ask at night to wake up there the following morning you will do so.

I asked, "Who is Jonathan?" and was told:

Jonathan is you. He is the part of you that you have been searching for, the true other half of your soul, the one true mate, your true marriage partner. You are just getting to know him and isn't he fine? When he and you are truly meshed the result will be a very beautiful human being. He is dignified but not stuffy, wise but not egotistic, fun loving but not silly, real and honest at all times and also very loving. He truly is beautiful. You have contacted stages of him before but never this deep of a stage. You are in for an enormous period of growth and prosperity. This is Mafu.

Jonathan is a master of the creation of the human being through the thought processes of the brain. You have always said you thought you were a master of creation because of the material that came through. You were only half right, the half of the soul incarnated with you. This is a new and expanded look at creation. You will really learn from this and at the same time be charting a new philosophy course for humanity. This will be the course of human brain wave patterns that will be very easy for all to follow.

This is Jonathan. The half of my soul on the manifested plane is truly a master of creation of the large universe. I, the half that stayed up to guide the incarnation am a master of the creation of the human being. You, Norma, the part of the seed core expressing on the earth, are a master of the combination because the halves of your soul are in the process of combining. This has been a long hard task for this integration to take place. We had to get you away from emotional turmoil. Just trust and let the universe take care of it. I am with you at all times now. I will not interfere unless I deem it appropriate. You must think of me as being inside your head, as indeed I am.

There are many facets being pulled together for our mission to begin. We want you to just have patience. There is a blending process between the two halves of your soul that must take place before the blended soul integrates completely with you the personality Norma. It is a process that can't be rushed. You will be directed at all times as to how to work with us in order for this to happen.

Asking For Personal Help

One morning I asked for personal help as follows: "I think I deserve some personal help this morning. I am at the point of making an important decision and I know that my higher self and my guidance system can see what's ahead and give me good solid advice. If they cannot do this then I would like to contact Abraham as it comes through Esther Hick's channel for personal help. I don't care which way it comes through because I need to have help. Please give me some good, practical, far-seeing advice on what you see as my direction. Thank you." I received the following:

This is Abraham wanting to speak with you. Esther is busy with other things at the moment so we have time to help. You are a valuable channel for the higher reaches of the Abraham Documentation Council as given before and, therefore, we feel you need to have help. We used to be the ones that came through you. Esther is focusing the energy on an area that she determined before entry would be her main concern. Therefore she is doing that which she determined to do and it is flowing mightily because she is in tune with her inner goals. You have not yet reached your inner goals. They are much advanced and therefore much harder to reach. It will be awhile yet before you discover your true mission. You are not into it yet. You need to concentrate on what really interests you.

You can do vocal channeling. We, Esther's channel will come through if the type of questions asked pertains to her focus. If they pertain to your visionary focus then the higher beings will come through. You see, the conglomerate will always answer from just exactly where each person is standing. Those attending Esther's workshops are all standing at the same place or they would not be in the audience. She is giving them just what they want and need to hear. This is what channeling is all about; this is what the conglomerate is about. It is the experiences of all those who have been through the earth plane processes. We are simply the coordinating group on this side of the dimensional division that edits and pulls together all this material, the same as you attempt to edit and pull together the material you contact on this side. We take the material we contact on your side and edit it and file it in the computer and what we give back then is what you edit and file, only it has been tempered by our editing and our insight into the psychological meaning of all that has happened or is happening on the earth in the mental thought of all, which is the conglomerate mind of the Creator.

When it was given that Chrysalis was the earth plane office of the Christ it was, at that time, seen to play the same function that the Abraham Documentary Council plays on this side. It can still play this role. You could conceivably pull together all inner plane channeling and coordinate it by pulling together terminology and making a complete picture. This is what we do. You have been given this thought before. You would be the perfect one to do the actual coordinating of all the channeled material because all parts of the Abraham conglomerate can come through you to give the coordinating terminology and pull the other thoughts into one cohesive concept for living life to the fullest. You can also continue to bring through the highest of the Abraham Teachings for the earth. On this side they are called the Abraham Teachings due to Abraham being the human tribe that populated the earth plane. This is the original tribe of human experience as opposed to animal experience. This is not to say that all on the earth plane are from the Abraham tribe, but if they are, then they are the true human, half man, half animal evolution.

When you see the total picture you will understand where you fit in that you can give the world the teachings from the earth plane view, the Chrysalis Teachings which is the office of the Christ on the earth plane – the Christ being that mind that is in all.

As given, the Abraham work on this side takes the mental thought processes of all who are out there experiencing and focuses them into certain areas. Even though other channels don't call themselves Abraham or Abdo, it is all from the same place. Esther Hicks as Abraham is focused on those who get what they want out of life and is turning what she sees on this side back to those who can make use of it in their lives. Other channels are doing the same. It is all the teachings that the Abraham Documentation Council pulls together. Those of you, then, on the earth plane are to pull all the channeled teachings together to give back to the earth and to us. In this way there is a round robin flow to things. Do you see why your mission is so very important?

The total pulling together of all channeled material is your true mission. The true pulling together of it will come through the Science of Music. You are seeing much too narrow a view of the Science of Music. It is the tying of everything into musical vibration to make communication easier between the inner and the outer. You need to think this through in your own mind and then we will expand on the picture more at a later date. It is a fantastic opportunity for the world, for humanity, for the Creator and especially for you and those that help you. You can't do it alone. No one can do it alone. Everyone needs to cooperate. Everyone needs to be acknowledged as to their importance in the overall picture. We simply must stop for today. Abdo and Council and all other Abraham Conglomerate beings available are standing by, cheering. We love you.

Approach to Channel Important

Yes, we are here as ever. We are always with you. We would like to discuss what you have to do to keep the door to us always open, instead of having to access us through the channeling, either by computer or vocal. We would just like to free flow about the channel, your channel and how to access it. Not only how others should access it but also how you can access it.

As far as how you can access it, the vocal channeling can be accessed at any time you start talking, but you must start the ball rolling. All you need to do is start explaining something that you think and it will kick in. It cannot be something that you've read that you're just repeating to others. It must be an original idea that you want to explain as your thoughts to others. It is at this time that the channel will kick in automatically. As repeated, you cannot take ideas as they come through others and expect your channel to kick in. You have an original first creation channel. It is not open to elaborate on other channel's material. There are channels that do this. They take all the channeled material that has come through others and regurgitate it. Esther Hick's channel is a pure original creation channel as is yours, but you will not bring through the same material as she does. The original creation channels are planned in the higher realms this way. We know what we are doing and would not take two precious channels and have them bring through the same material. This would not make sense to us.

As far as how others should approach your channel, circumstances must be right for the channel to come through. Those approaching your channel need to ask the questions with the attitude of a child. To begin with you, Norma, are a very simple mental make-up as far as thought processes go and you need to be approached from the position a child would take when asking his parents or his teachers a question. They need to be still open to learning and not have closed their minds or not have preset ideas of their own as to what the answer should be. Anyone who comes to you with preset thoughts on the answers will close you off. They must trust your channel, which means they must trust you. They should have respect for people in general. This is the attitude needed for your channel to feel comfortable.

Remember that you are to keep the questions simple and any who ask questions of you must simplify them. We cannot get clarity with a muddled up mind to bring through that which they will understand. In other words, they must simplify what the question, the basic bare bones question, is in their own mind and then we can reach them, answer that and then elaborate and most likely answer the more complicated aspects of their thoughts. But if they bring a complicated philosophical question to the table they will not receive the answer. Great channels have always taught this way; even the one called Jesus the Christ.

This is where it must start is with your self-confidence and your appearance and the way you come across to others. You must be seen as whole. When you are truly able to stand on your own and bring through all parts of yourself comfortably, then all will change. For the time being know that you have much help at this time from everyone. Yes, you have taken another step forward and you are finding your curiosity and your determination.

There are other considerations on our side of the veil also. One of them is whether we are available, or refuse to come forward due a lack of sincere interest on the channel's part. The channel's attitude will stop the information from being available. The channel has to be sincerely interested in bringing it through at the time they try or it simply will not be available. You see, we know whether or not that interest is there and will simply not come through if it isn't there. The channel's own attitude is as important as anyone else's.

For instance, the solar project has been stopped for several years now and to bring through material for it again you need to stay focused on it in your own mind. You will have to become interested in the solar project again and prime the pump in order to have the ability to bring it through. Questions from others will help, but if you, yourself, aren't vitally interested you will not receive the information. It is going to be something you'll have to concentrate on for a period of time to start the flow up again because of your lack of practice at reaching the higher energies. You will have to build up your energy by degrees. Why not lay out a series of clarifying questions on your own and see if you can get the ball rolling once again. We know it is there and we know you can reach it, but you have to really want to with all your heart and soul.

At one point Mafu came through and said that my channeling group would slant the advice on the solar to suit their wishes. This upset me and I asked if this was why I'm caught always in duality? Is it because I channel my own background and knowledge and experience and then I channel from the higher planes and it is at odds?" I asked if they could please explain about this. Which one was I supposed to listen to? I said that I would think a person should follow their own channeling system, their own guidance, but is this only true if that person can't reach those from the higher realms? I said I was really confused on this issue and perhaps if someone from the very highest realms could explain this to me it would help me see the direction I am supposed to go. It wasn't that I didn't agree with what Mafu said – I did, but there is another part of me that said that is not the way for me to go to gain strength of my own character, that that is the way of dependency again. If this is true, and the solar project needs to be done with others, I asked what was I supposed to do or accomplish on my own to give me the feeling of accomplishment and of independence that I need to feel, to help me be the real me. I asked about the timing as far as the solar project? I channeled that now was the time, but was this my channel or the higher realms

151

channel? I asked for help. The following reply came through:

We see your solar project in the fourth dimension along with most all your other work. Therefore, it will always be impossible for us to give a time on it. As far as your thoughts on someone buying your channel, we want you to realize that no one can buy your channel. No one can buy you. For one thing, you are too strong internally to let that happen and we are your internal self guarding against that. We simply will not cooperate if anyone tries to manipulate you in this way. Do you understand? There is no way anyone can buy your channel. They can influence the fifteen percent or so that is the personal Norma coming through, but that is all. You must strengthen this part of the channel so there is no longer any need to let this happen.

We have given what we can. We are afraid that it is not what you hoped. You see, we also have a difficult time with the movement of time as far as giving you time lines for anything to happen. We must determine whether we are seeing and interpreting in third or fourth dimension. Things in the third dimension are much more accurate. What we see in the fourth is open to much error as far as time.

We are going to take you to one higher than Abdo. Abdo, himself, is one of the highest archangels, and the others in your channeling group are also of the highest and finest ability, each in their own way. You must at all times know that you can depend on them.

At the present time Abdo wishes to state that the solar project is very important and needs to have the cooperation of his beautiful children. It has to be a teamwork project. You will not let some messages into your consciousness through stubbornness which we hope you will soon overcome. Regardless, these messages are then sent through another who is unaware that he is channeling them and us, but channeling he is. The project that can be to your satisfaction of accomplishing will be your books. This must remain as your own thing. From these projects will come your sense of fulfillment. You will also have this sense of fulfillment from the solar if you will overcome the stubbornness.

When Mafu said that they had their own point of wish, or their own wishes, he meant that they would slant the view from their excitement and anticipation etc. from the tenth plane of experimentation. What happens is that the spiritual growth of the individual is not uppermost in the mind of the information that comes from the tenth plane. This is why much of your material deals with science and not as much with spirituality. Those coming through you from the tenth plane are very strong and this is why your interest is in this area more so than the spiritual. But at the same time there are the others in your channeling group that have the responsibility of monitoring your spiritual growth, knowing that in the long run this is more important than getting the solar project done. It is, you know. At the present time your spiritual growth has been phenomenal. We want to see that it continues to be because we know that in the long run this is the only way this project can be accomplished.

The difference between channeling your own group or guidance system and that of the higher planes has no bearing in your case because your own channeling group is from the highest planes. The concern comes in the area of interest and which particular member of your channeling group you are accessing. Perhaps it would be wise to always check each communication out at the end with comments from Abdo, who will give them from the spiritual viewpoint. At that time, then, you will need to bring into play your own judgment and decision making process if there is anything that seems to be at odds or if there is a difference of opinion about something.

CHAPTER 9

CONTACT WITH THE MUSICAL UNIVERSE

66Here's a picture I really like because of being a musician." I said to Neil.

"It certainly is weird, isn't it?" Neil asked.

We had taken walk on the Third Street Promenade in Santa Monica. It was quite an experience. This was a picture of a statue outside one of the stores.

Santa Monica Statue

"What about this statue appeals to you anyway?" Neil

asked.

"Well a lot of my material has to do with the Science of Music (to be given in a later notebook) and also the TimeTraveler has a pretty good explanation of the time when I was practicing vocal channeling and I reached the Musical Universe," I answered. I guess this statue just kind of brought back that channeling session; Notice the treble clef sign for a face. Maybe I drew a picture in my mind of what the entities looked like and they have looked something like this. I really don't know – all I know is I liked it. Let's tune into what the session was like; it's pretty interesting," I replied.

Practicing Vocal Channeling

I had not tried to vocal channel for a long time and I decided to try it one afternoon. In fact, I hadn't been channeling at all for many reasons. I had been studying many different disciplines, the latest being The Pathwork. Regardless, approximately five years later the following came through the channeling:

Higher Self Channeling

Yes, we are here this afternoon with you. It has been a long time, you are correct, since we have tried to vocal channel. This is your channel – you, your higher self coming through at the moment. We will eventually turn it over to others including Mafu, who can help and perhaps he will turn it on over then to the Musical Universe. This is your central channel, the central core of your being. You are having a spiritual crisis, indeed, because of stubbornness in your ego makeup.

The Pathwork is accurate material; you have felt this from the beginning. It rang a bell with you so you know it is accurate material. It is, at this time and place in your life, something for you to steady you, to give direction to your inner growth. You are in contact with your inner being, which is the whole idea of the meditation processes, etc. and for this reason you do not need to have that part of it, but you need to have the steadiness of knowing that there is a path that is logical and true and that you can follow, that you're not entirely tossed out into the ocean of storms with nowhere to turn and no one who has ever been through this before. Many, many, many people have been through this spiritual crisis that you are in the midst of. The crisis is partly due to the frustration that you feel which is due to the fact that you're no longer tapping into your own channel. And your own channel is not necessarily just me. Your own channel is all the way up – every level all the way up to the Creator God. This is the direction that we would like to see your work take, is tying in the big, large, macro universe processes to those of the human brain, because this truly is the path of progress of the human brain. If one is understood the other will be understood and we would sincerely like to see you focus on this.

As far as channeling in public, yes you are capable. You have always been capable and for this reason we believe that the Anthony Robbins work is good for you, as is the Pathwork and we heartily agree that you stay on both these courses for the time being because the Anthony Robbins material is making you realize that you need to speak up, that you can speak up in front of people. You could speak up tonight at this meeting if you so desired. If it would make you feel better we will assure you that Mafu will come through or one of the higher beings from the musical realm will come through and be there. But it's not necessary because your higher self has all this knowledge within itself.

You have the total Science of Music, the total creation of the universe at your disposal as you yourself, without an outside entity channeling through you. And there is nothing wrong with having an outside entity channel through you. It takes a little more energy, perhaps. There is absolutely nothing wrong with it and if you want the Abraham Documentary Council to come through you we will do that if you would sincerely like to get started doing public channeling. We will guarantee that you will be an overnight success which would also lead to financial success which would also lead to the completion of all your projects. So the way to get started, Miss Norma, is to just book a lecture and then ask for questions at the end of the lecture. This is a format that we feel you would be comfortable with – calling it a lecture instead of an open forum because the questions seem to be what is sticking you for the moment. What you seem to be the most concerned about is your ability to answer these questions. You have that ability. You have every guarantee. Every insurance policy you could possibly have, you've got. In fact, much more so than other channels that are out there putting their necks on the line, if that's the way you want to say it.

We are turning you over now to the Abraham Documentation Council. Your channel is coming through very, very strong and when they come through the energy will be much stronger and you may not be able to handle it for as long as you would if I continue. This is one reason why, when you give a lecture, that if you use your own channel to do the answering your energy will hold up much, much longer than if you use the Abraham Council. We are going to turn you over now to the Abraham Council. Please take one moment to center yourself and allow these beautiful beings to come through your body, which will also be a healing process for you. Yes, you could talk this way at all times to everyone if you just decide that's what you want to do. It's entirely up to you Miss Norma. I'm calling you Miss Norma because that's what the children call you when you teach and you're used to hearing it and you respond to it with a beautiful glow because of the children. So in our meditation periods – one more moment before I turn you over – in our meditation periods if you hear Miss Norma coming through the thought processes you will know that I am there because this is what I intend to call you. Thank you.

Abraham Documentation Council Channeling

Yes, this is the Abraham Documentation Council. As your higher self indicated, we are available at any time to answer questions when you give lectures. As far as the creation material we see it published as a pamphlet or book, whichever is deemed the best course on the earth plane. And we also see it as a lecture combined with your music. You've been receiving the right impression on that.

The musical play that you have written is an exoteric area which your higher self can help you with as far as advice on it is concerned. That is not for us to enter into. The best way for you to earn your living at this moment would be to start doing your lectures. And so you start small, say you start with four people, but it will gain momentum as you gain confidence and maturity.

Your higher self is much more highly evolved than your personality – your lower self. The Abraham material touches your lower self and helps steady it. The Pathwork material touches you, your personality and will steady it and the Abraham Documentation Council works with your higher self. It is one and the same channel. And the three different paths are for your three different individual aspects that you are working on. Your higher self is much more highly evolved than either of the other two, although the personality is gaining and coming into alignment. The lower self has not yet fallen into alignment with the personality. This is the stage, right at the moment that you need to focus on, Miss Norma. And we are calling you Miss Norma, too, although we are not your higher self, but we like the sound of it.

Archangels Channeling

Good day from the archangels overseeing Abdo and council. We do not ordinarily give advice to any on this level, but have made an exception in your case. And now, we're going to turn you over to the part that the guide from the Pathwork channeled from – the type of material that he channeled from and we will continue to call him the guide for Pathwork even though it is a conglomerate also. Know you this.

Pathwork Guide Channeling

The guide from the Pathwork is with us and he wishes to address you. Yes, he was with you in your last session, but it is not the actual Pathwork guide, it is a layer of the Documentation Council. The guide giving the Pathwork material was not an individual. That material was also from the Abraham Documentation Council. At the time that Miss Eva was doing the channeling for the Pathwork material it was deemed best to just sign it as the guide. Therefore the "Pathwork guide," so to speak, has moved on and is not available for contact. When Miss Eva passed over, the re-connection was made and they are moving along together. The same thing takes place with each person who is bringing through the channel. The channel is part of them. At times you may contact a wisp of this guide that is left here in the inner beings of others who were associated with her. This is what is taking place when you are told it is the Pathwork guide. Part of the Pathwork guide is the divine mind as is part of every channel and that part is still available to be reached, but the main concentration of energy that came through Miss Eva is reunited with her and has moved beyond the planes where you can contact it. She was a very highly evolved master as are you. You just have not accepted your mastership as she did. You realize that you are both in the arts. This is the point that needs to be stressed in all that you do.

We are a much calmer part of the conglomerate and welcome you with open arms to this material. We are not going, at this time, to go into any revisions or updates on the Pathwork material. Basically it is still the same. What we would like to do is align it with your personality which

161

(you just received this information), is where it will do the most good. Your higher self does not need to have this material. It has long since passed it up. Your lower self is not ready for it although it is coming into line to be ready for it. That is what the Pathwork is all about, is to align all aspects of you and it must start with what we call the middle you, the personality you. The Pathwork will bring the lower self and all aspects of it into alignment with the reality of your life. By aspects we mean attitudes that you have about certain facets of your life that need to be brought into alignment. One of these attitudes is the martyr in you that makes you feels like you've been shortchanged by life. You have not! You have a glorious inner being. You have not been shortchanged! You are in absolutely the most fantastic place that anyone could be as far as reaching your inner being. Therefore, the Pathwork for you will be working on those attitudes of yours that are blocking your progress (your behavior). It will show these attitudes to you along with your ability to bring into line these other aspects of you. Your separation from other people is one of the aspects that need to be brought into alignment with the reality of you now.

The reality of you now is not Chrysalis any longer and this is what you must realize. You are no longer the Chrysalis Foundation. You have passed that work up. That work still needs to get out, we're not saying that it's invalid; we're just saying that the circumstances that were given to you to start a Chrysalis Foundation are no longer in place. You have moved on. The people who were involved with you have moved on. The separateness that you are holding onto is your biggest blockage. We believe that we have kept the channel open long enough for the time being. We are being told, yes, that the musical universe would like to

162

have a chance to bring through something that they would like to speak to you about, so here we go...

Musical Universe Channeling

Yes, we are the Musical Universe. It has been a long time since we have had the opportunity to convey our best wishes to you. This is what we would like to do at the moment, is to remind you that we are here ever ready to bring through updates of the Science of Music. Your thoughts that have been recently on the Personal Music Charts are because we are trying to influence you to bring through more material on these Personal Music Charts which could also be a viable way for you to earn your living. You have so much that you can do that we have no idea why you despair so at times. But we do want you to know that we are ever in your aura and ready when you are. This is all we will give for today. Thank you. We're going to turn you back to your higher self at the present time.

Higher Self Channeling

Yes, Miss Norma, you're going back and forth on the channel which is good practice. This is what we want to do. This is what is needed is to be able to go to any one of these channels at any time and bring through the information called for. Right now, we want to tap into Abraham and bring him through to give his idea of how the Abraham material can help you the most.

Abraham Channeling

Yes, good day. The way the Abraham material can help you, and we're also going to call you Miss Norma, the way this material can help you at the present time is to keep your lower part, the part that has its feet stuck in the concrete on the earth plane, to keep it focused and balanced. This can be done with knowing that there is a part of you, the Norma part of you that has a fantastic life to lead over and above and beyond what your channel is. The personality you is what the Abraham material will help with. Therefore, we want to see you continue this work. You can handle it all. It's been outlined for you, the three different areas of your beingness and the three different paths to use on it. How much luckier can a person get than you. You've got it all. So we expect great things to come from all of this. The Anthony Robbins material is fine for that part of you. To bring the alignment of your lower self into that is where we intend to help. We want to let you know that it's okay to want things, and it's okay, not only okay but absolutely necessary, to focus on this wanting. At that time, when you focus on it and want it so bad, this is when Anthony Robbins material will work. And once the Anthony Robbins material starts working then comes the higher realms of the Abraham Council working with your higher self. We see that within a short time your life is going to be totally changed if you cooperate with all the help that's being given you. There are plans for you to be a very influential channel in the days to come. Now we don't very often give material like this, but at the same time that you're to be an influential channel, you can also have all

164

that you want on a personal level. It can both happen at the same time. In fact, it must happen at the same time. The beautiful channel cannot happen until the beautiful personality is pulled into alignment with the lower part. When that happens everything you want as a personality will happen.

We want you to continue with the Abraham work, we mean the pure Abraham work such as the tapes and personal sessions if you wish, with Abraham, such as you're doing today. The biggest benefit would be to get more tapes and be sure to listen to those tapes. But basically you know the principles; the biggest thing is to just simply apply the principles by doing your positive aspects and by doing your writing. You can do this whether or not you go to the meetings. The meetings are fine. They are good for you; they get you out in public. Now the energy is going fast and we feel that we must quit. One last pass through your higher mind, back into your personality level, hopefully not any lower than that, down into your lower self. Try to stay centered into your personality level up towards your higher level. Thank you.

Higher Self Channeling

Yes, Miss Norma, this is your higher self, your inner being, the core of beingness for you. We think you've done a fantastic job here today and we hope you will continue practicing because the opportunity is going to come soon to use all that you are capable of using. Thank you and good day. We love you. All of us love you, all the way up. There is nothing wrong with you dear child. You had a bad upbringing, which was not the fault of either of your parents. They had a bad upbringing. It is simply the residue of all humanity and you have got to clean it out. You have got to pull it up and clean it out. Then the channel will be pure. This is where the Pathwork will come in. The Abraham material, as given before, will keep you focused on what it is you want with your feet on the earth plane. It will help you keep down to reality. The Pathwork is where your work is for the moment. Thank you and good day.

I Will Always Have Channel

I was told after this that even though there may be times when I don't do much channeling I will not lose the channel, I cannot lose it, as it is a part of me now and will ever be. It may get rusty and need to be primed, but will ever be there.

On a recent occasion I opened the channel and asked for inspiration and information that would allow me to gradually enter into effective and enlightening channeling. I asked for comments on anything that would enlighten me and humanity on what channeling is and how it works and where the information was coming from. I received the following:

Contact with the Synthesized Channel from the Middle of the Head

Yes, this is your synthesized channel from the middle of the head. We are glad to have a chance to communicate. First we believe that a book should be pulled together from your material. We believe you should do this, not someone else, because you will be able to receive many insights when the material is put into logical order. There is a very definite order to the channeling process. It involves three areas of the brain. As given before, you first access your past incarnations when the channel opens, then you progress to your present time period of teachers, which would include your own soul on the inner planes, then you progress to your future incarnations. All of your previous incarnations, and your present one, have had a hand in giving birth to these future incarnations. You do not access just one future incarnation, as there is an order to them also. You will access the nearest one to your time span of the present first. Then you will progress.

In your case, your nearest incarnation is Donoray and the Science of Music. He also is the keeper and inventor of the solar project. If this does not take place in this incarnation it will most certainly do so in the next. It would be an interesting experiment to leave a record of your expectancy of coming back as Donoray. Your next incarnation after that is in an embryo stage at this time. It will be more completely formed by the rest of this experience plus the next one of Donoray. We cannot say for sure what its accomplishments will be as that depends, as already given, on what Donoray and you accomplish this life and the next. But it is inside your brain as an embryo and what takes place now and in the next life will form what it will be. There is never more than one that is receiving completion progress at a time as far as incarnations on the earth plane. You also have beings that are part of your past, present and future on many other planes of dimension.

Channeling does come from both outside entities and within the human brain (the presently manifested entity itself). We would like to clear this up as much as possible. We are your synthesized brain which includes all your past, present and future beings into one channel. This is intuition. Please know us as the Keepers of Intuition. We will not give names, there simply are too many. Know that it is simply Norma.

We are with you at all times, remember. As a matter of fact, we are expressing more and more as part of your personality, even when you are not aware of it. This is the process of growth of the channel. This is the way it is supposed to work. No one should be able to tell when it is you, as the personality Norma they've known all along, or whether it is the new parts of your personality expressing through the old. We are the parts that have been allowed eternal life and the ability to be part of any incarnation you have from this point on if it is desired that we be a part.

There is a possibility that in some future incarnation you would wish to incarnate without us, either to learn some particular lesson or to further your growth for a major step ahead. If it is determined that you want to serve the rest of humanity more than to work on your own lessons, then we will be part of the incarnation. We are the humanitarians of the planet. You have given birth to us by allowing us the expression through the channel at limited times. It is a natural growth process that we will become you and the channel will be open at all times to bring through the wisdom of the ages to help your fellow man. If this channel is abused and used to serve personal needs or wishes or desires we will withdraw as an automatic process because our sole purpose is to help humanity evolve.

We want to give this because of the doubts you expressed at the last vocal channeling session as to whether it was you or us. It is both and will continue to be both. This is the proper way for channeling to eventually evolve. Yes there's still a little tipsiness as we walk. When you take better care of your form, through diet and exercise, this will not be so. Thank you for your cooperation. I will stay with you for a while longer.

We're asking the channel to relax for a moment. She's becoming nervous. The process that is taking place with the channel is that when speaking what she is getting, it is a much faster process than typing it. The speech is going faster than what she is bringing through can be given at this stage. It just is a matter of practice. She is used to having a slight bit more time to analyze the thought forms and pictures as they are given to her and while she is typing them, she's pondering the next picture or thought that is coming in. With the process of speaking, all the mechanism has been speeded up and she is not processing what is being given to her fast enough. Therefore, expect some pauses. We will not have her turn the recording machine off the next time; we will just let her pause.

We feel we must close now and not take advantage of the energy of Ms. Norma's body any longer. We do require high voltage to operate from our position and we will turn this back over to Ms. Norma so she can return to normal operating power. She is indeed feeling the waves of the high energy. It distorts her impression of, or perception of, space, seeming to squeeze her head into a narrow package. At the same time there seems to be regular pulsations coming from the right eye. We are having her describe this from her perspective before we shut down the energy. Her head is beginning to ache now in the left area of the forehead. This is enough. Good day.

Explanation of the Synthesized Channel

The synthesized channel is the one in the center of her head. This is the opening of her God Within with the conglomerate mind and the divine mind blended together for an overall picture that is made up of past present and future. She is the present, the conglomerate mind is the past and the divine mind is the future. (You could compare this with the story of "Scrooge and the ghosts of Christmas past, present and future.")

This is what each human needs to do is to carry a synthesized picture of himself with him at all times. This will be the result of "meditation" and "daydreaming" and being "present in the moment." It takes all three to have a well-rounded human being. The prospect of a human's life when they do not combine these three very essential mental processes is very bleak and dreary. This is the focal point of the new philosophy that we mentioned to Norma several months ago that she would be bringing onto the earth plane. We are from the musical universe which no one else on the earth plane is tapping into as a part of the conglomerate mind. We are, all of us, musicians from previous incarnations of people incarnated on the earth at the present time.

You, Norma, are noticing pressure in the left, right and top sides of your head. You are using the synthesized channel which combines all three areas of channeling. At times you will only be using one of the three or two of the three. At the moment, all channels are wide open on you. This is the "living library" that is available to everyone. The head librarian is one that knows which part of the channel to access to receive certain information. This is the training period you are in now. We would wish that it could progress faster and we see a time period in the immediate future when it will progress faster.

We want to thank this channel for this rare opportunity to bring this information through and to, at the same time, show her what her synthesized channel is capable of. She has been using the center of the head for this channeling, the blended right and left and center and it has worked very nicely. We would like to encourage her to continue tapping into this part of the channel several times a week. She was told to not channel for at least six months while this blending took place, but her progress has been so rapid that we deem it okay for her to continue channeling.

The Musical Universe

Several years ago I had a transmission from a group who called themselves the Musical Universe. They came through the vocal channeling one day and said that I was the first one they had ever been able to have contact with on the earth plane. They told me that I have the total Science of Music, the total creation of the universe at my disposal within myself, without an outside entity channeling through me.

From the Musical Universe:

We are from the musical universe which no one else on the earth plane is tapping into as a part of the conglomerate mind. We are, all of us, musicians from previous lives of people incarnated on the earth at the present time. We have never before had the opportunity to convey our best wishes to you. This is what we would like to do at the moment, and to remind you that we are here ready to bring through updates on the Science of Music. We want you to know that we are ever in your aura and ready to help. The musical universe is the last one that you go into before getting into the area where thought processes are refined over and over again all the way into that Holy Sphere inside your mind.

We want to thank you for this rare opportunity to bring information through. We are from the musical universe which is where the origins of your mastership are located – your roots, in other words. Your true mastership is the knowledge of how the perfect human being was created. My name is Marlo.

I, Norma, had never heard of Marlo until this came through. Once after that he ended a transmission as follows:

This is Marlo and friends from the musical universe. Know you that I am music personified as are all of those with me. I am asexual and have moved past the stage of being part of any composition, but have been through all of the compositions that have ever been played on the planet earth from the beginning of time.

Being from the Musical Universe means that we are the cells in Norma's body that have been given birth by means of musical vibration. We were encoded into the physical form that she entered, before she, as the spirit, entered this form. Our growth has followed with music as nourishment ever since we opened up at the age of four. This particular form was specially encoded to allow an opening of the musical cells of all the previous experience with music that this entity Norma has had, to be readily available in this lifetime. Thus the growth and evolvement of these cells has been taking place ever since their opening at the age of four. These musical cells are where the information about the previous work on the Science of Music that has been done on the inner planes is stored. Even now, this work is ongoing and the work done at night is stored in the cells waiting for her to catch up to it. Thank you and good day."

I was told that the Musical Universe also handles material from the past along with future technology. This explains why the information on the original seven universes that I was given in Volume I of the notebooks, "The TimeLine of Eternity," was given in relationship to musical tones and the colors associated with them (the colors of the rainbow matching the C major scale).

CHAPTER 10

THE SYNTHESIZED CHANNEL

"I always liked this picture you took of Rifle Falls in Colorado," I said to Neil. Actually I wish it showed more of the stream that the falls flow into. You can see a little of it, but not much," I continued.

Rifle Falls - Rifle, Colorado

"It was hard to get the top of the falls and also get the bottom all in the same picture," Neil said. "I do wish it showed more of the stream at the bottom?" Neil answered.

"At one point the TimeTraveler compared the channeling to three lines feeding into our brain and coming out as one composite line. This picture kind of shows this except I would like to see more of the one line, or stream, coming out at the bottom," I answered.

"Oh well, I did my best," Neil said, laughing. "Let's find out what all the TimeTraveler had to say about it," he continued.

The Synthesized Channel

There is one point we wish to bring out. When the channel comes through the left side of your head it is an outside entity. When the energy comes through and is felt on the right side – as it is now – it is from within your beingness. When it comes through the center it is the blending of your personality and your inner being. Remember this. Left side - outside entity; right side - core of your being; center - blended personality and inner being. You are asking what the difference is between the core of your being and your inner being. The difference is the core of your being possesses all the knowledge and memories that you have experienced from time immemorial. The inner being that blends with the personality is made up of energies on the inner planes that you and all others have put there. The inner being, as spoken of by Abraham, is this conglomerate inner being made up of your thought and the thoughts of all others. The outside entities are, of course, personalities of yours from the past or the future. Also at times you do contact personalities of others who are working in this particular realm of spiritual mission on this side of the veil. Where this material is coming from at the moment is within the core of your beingness as what you have learned throughout the ages in your many incarnations. The three lines feeding in should blend into one composite line coming out of you at all times, whether spoken or written.

When you want to write beautiful music, you should access the right side of the computer (brain). When you want to bring in future technology you should access the left. When wanting to bring in current events and prophesy and psychological behavior of humans and what can help at the present time for all to grow, you access the center of your receiving station. Remember, right, left and center.

For your own personal help you need to first access the right side, then the left side, then the center. The way this works is you access what you brought in to work on and the strengths you brought in to draw on, then you go to former and future personalities for what worked in the past and what you want as a goal in the future. At that time you access the center and see how all this information fits in and meshes with other humans you are associated with and what they may be needing – how you can help them while helping yourself, and what would be good as a method to help others, etc. We believe you are beginning to get the idea. Let us experiment. Concentrate right now on only the right side of your head. Only allow messages from this side and for energy from this side to be active.

Your thoughts are how does this tie in with your chart of the divisions of the brain. The right side is the emotional body, the left the mental and the center the spiritual. Any interaction with others in your life is considered your spirituality. This is something that many don't consider. The other three divisions are personal growth only. This is all they are concerned with. Even teachings that come through are for personal growth until you reach the fourth division which is the center. Your left side and your center are very well developed, but not your right side. This is the area that needs to be concentrated on. This is why we are advocating a return to your music, especially performing and composing, not necessarily the teaching. We believe this is enough this morning. At the present time you have moved the energy to the center which will not help you access your inner core. Please try one more time to bring a small portion of insight through from the right side. Remember how the right side felt when it first opened up? That was pure wisdom and insight from the very center of your being in an esoteric manner. It is all stored there. If you truly want to reach personal happiness and fulfillment this is the side you need to concentrate on. The others can then be accessed easily. This side cannot be accessed that easily. It is like you skipped grades in school and need to back track to make them up. We believe that music will be the quickest and best way. Now try and bring though a simple description of love for us:

Love is a feeling a bird gets sitting on her nest waiting for the eggs to hatch. She is patient and content knowing that the inspiration and instigation of the process of creation has taken place and is quite content to rest while awaiting the birth of the products of creation. She feels secure in knowing that her job is temporarily on hold until nature (or the universe) deems it time to expose the creation to the manifested world.

That was very good. Now see how this applies to your own situation. You have had the inspiration and went through the instigation. Now is the time to just sit on the nest resting patiently until nature (or the universe) sees that it is time to expose the creation to the manifested world. At that time the mother bird's duties of job or mission will begin again in earnest by needing to feed and care for her young. When the time comes that they can fly on their own and fly away to become entities in their own right, then mother bird is free to start another family. The hatching of the egg of the solar project is to be more compared with that of the gestation of an elephant, but the process is still the same. The mother bird does not lose interest in the eggs while awaiting the hatching. She is ever conscious of protecting them and keeping them warm. But at the same time she is content to occupy her mind with other things such as improving her nest, taking turns with the father bird at sitting on the eggs, etc. When you follow nature everything will flow much better.

Apply this same concept to your relationships and to other problem areas in your life. If the inspiration and instigation stages have been achieved then let the eggs hatch in their own time, but be very protective of them and let no harm come to them from negative influences. When the right time comes they will hatch into the manifested place instead of the unmanifested, where they are now. This has been Mafu as a helper for the channel of Norma.

Yes, we are here though it is difficult for you to feel us. We seem quite dim to you. This is due in part to a slight ear infection which does affect your communication because part of the process of channeling is done through the inner ear. When the inner ear canal is infected it dims the transmission. But we are here. Your health problems will clear up soon. Remember to protect yourself at all times against everyone.

Others can receive messages from your cells. There can be a cellular bonding between two people that is more binding than any physical bonding. It is possible to have this bonding with everyone you are associated with if they are spiritually advanced. They can receive the very same information because they use your body as the transformer. They will do this until their own system is more complete. When this takes place, you will be able to receive from them. As it is now you do not receive from others that are at a lower level.

You, Miss Norma, can play an important role in this progress. You are a master educator and a master creationist and you need to combine the two and further this knowingness on the earth plane in order to fulfill your plans for this incarnation which have been in the making for the last several incarnations.

At certain times the timing is right for all of your projects if started at that particular time, to be an instantaneous success. This is due to many reasons, one of them being astrological. We realize you don't understand the ins and outs of the astrological charts so we will not get into it. Just know that the stars guiding and directing your life are in perfect alignment at certain times for all that your mission will cover. This business of planets being in alignment affects all parts of your life. The further you go on the spiritual path the more bearing astrological charts have on your progress. This is especially true for those born on the cusp. You, Norma, are on the cusp, not only of a new age, but of a season and of a month. Also, your moon was on a cusp. You chose all this for the contrasting negative and positive. Without the pull of these two back and forth there would be no friction and it is friction that instigates growth. There must be the friction which pushes you up another rung of the ladder in your growth and progress.

Opening the Channel in Children

The use of the channel needs to be prepared from the day of birth onward to operate in the fully developed human as it should. This is the ultimate goal of the school material which will be discussed in a future volume of the notebooks. This material is valid and viable as a preparatory method for opening the channel early in children.

The first cracks in the channel will come through the dreams of children as flashes back to previous lives. Some may be good flashes and some may be scary but all are important and children should be trained to remember and record these dreams as soon as they are old enough to talk. These dreams will give indications of past skills and of conflicts that were never resolved. The skills will come as happy dreams, the conflicts as bad dreams, to simplify things. This will also hold true for adults. A dream that shows them exhibiting a feat that they have not accomplished in this life means that they did accomplish it in some other life. This holds true up to a certain point on the channel. This is the work on the lower right side of the brain diagram.

The work on the upper left side will progress to present time period incarnations which will include the period of the last two thousand years. This is all considered the present age. This will also have its stages. Remember that all entities re-circulate and those that you contact in the channel at this point are quite often who you were in some recent past incarnations. To clarify, children's dreams can quite often show them as flowers, birds or animals or perhaps back even further as rocks and stones. This is part of the child's fascination with rocks and stones and plants and animals. This is why the different play grounds in the experimental school (to be discussed in a future volume of the notebooks) will be incorporated into the learning process. This is where their dreams are going to be located to begin with. The memory cycle of the brain will follow evolution. It is as simple as that.

To return to what we were discussing, if you contact a Biblical character it is possible that you were this character if you are one of the main sprouts of the seed core. If you are not, then you were most definitely associated with this character.

To explain main sprouts of the seed core, when the spark split upon landing and the energy separated into male and female, there was one identity or consciousness left that then splintered smaller sparks off from it. There will always be the main entity and splinters that will be re-circulating together for the most part. The main entity is the one that makes the most progress in each life and also does the most to help other humans in their growth. If the time of Moses comes to you in dreams or regressions, then you either were Moses or one of the splinter sparks off the main entity who was Moses. No one knows for sure if he is the main consciousness or one of the splinter consciousness's because the relationship is so close that one feels like the other. This is an inner bond felt by seed core groups. Most often, the oversoul or main entity, does not even incarnate, only in certain time periods, and all those on the earth are the splinter sparks. This is just another way of putting it to help with understanding.

Adolescence and Mid-Life Crises

The upper left section of the brain diagram is in contact with all the present incarnations. These are the teachers and guides and the other half of your soul that is not incarnated. They are all to be found in this section. Contact with this section aids and serves a human's progress from early adulthood to middle age. Contact with lower evolutionary forms served from birth to adulthood. The change over from section one of the brain to section two for the inner life is the period known as adolescence when turmoil is gone through, and the period known as mid-life crises when another period of turmoil is gone through is the change over from section two to section three. Needless to say, the more contact with the inner life, the easier these time periods will be. The stress that the physical body goes through at these times would be eased. There would be an elimination of mood swings that are common in both periods. As a matter of fact, the tantrums and behavior of a child in "the terrible twos" would be considerably different if the child could express, or is allowed to express his dreams and not be hushed up and ridiculed or considered unimportant. Everything a child feels at this point should be allowed expression and given consideration as important aspects of what is going to make up his personality and what his life pursuit is going to be about.

The Upper Right or Spiritual Section of Brain

The next section of the brain, the upper right should open up when the strife of raising children and pushing so hard to earn a living recedes. This will bring the time needed to allow the opening into the upper right section, the spiritual section. This is when the actual work begins that will be preparatory for planning the next incarnations, or perhaps we should say finalizing the preparations for the immediate next incarnation and beginning to form ones after that.

The contacts that are made in the spiritual section of the channel are from enlightened beings that are not part of your beingness, your consciousness, because you have not yet progressed to this level. They are there to help you aspire to this level, to help you try to make the change over into spiritual thought and spiritual importance to all parts of your life. You can never become one of these spiritual beings because they are those sparks who never fell and split the energy into positive and negative, as is your background.

We want to make this perfectly clear. Those of you incarnated on the earth plane can never become one of the high spiritual beings that you contact at this point because you are from the evolutionary worlds and they are from the spiritual worlds. This is why the channeling that comes from them is not as applicable in everyday practical terms as is the channeling from the section below this one. They have never incarnated on the earth and never will. If you contact one who has been incarnated on the earth, know you that this spirit is from the upper left section of the brain map, not the upper right. The entities from the spiritual section, the upper right, help you form your next incarnations; they give insight on how things work in the spiritual worlds and aid and abet those who try to step higher plane concepts down to earth.

Different Ways to Help With Channeling

At one point I asked if anyone could recommend any particular exercises or music that I should do while practicing the piano to get the most benefit and help with bringing through the channeling. I received the following:

You recently went into a deeper state of channeling, almost a trance channeling. This is the first time this had happened. Your conscious mind was thinking of something entirely different while we were writing something else. This is the result of the NLP (neuro-linguistic programming) that was used on you this past weekend. Some more intense training in this area would be of great benefit to the channel. What it does is allow the channeling process to feed in while the everyday state is being maintained. This would be of great benefit to vocal channeling the proper way. Most vocal channels are not doing this. They are, indeed in a trance, which is not the correct way, although some trance channels are much closer to the real goal than most others. You have the ability to do this and this would be the proper function of the channel – to do unconscious receiving while talking to other people, using the material that comes in. This way it is much more relevant to the conversation that is taking place.

Some sessions with one who is advanced in energy work would do a lot to clear out your channel. Your channel is quite clear, we're not saying it is contaminated; it just would make the whole process much easier. You see how you're weaving back and forth while doing vocal channeling. This means that the physical body is under stress to bring this through and this is what we are giving – that energy-wise you would not have this, you would have the ease that others have in vocal channeling. If more of this energy work was done and more of these blockages were cleared out and then your diet was improved, you would be well able to bring vocal channeling through at ease.

You can and should do the exercise of cross weaving your brain (given in a previous volume). It is something that should be done daily along with whatever clearing you do of your chakras and the breathing exercise. It should be made a part of your morning routine as far as setting your temperature guide – your thermostat guide.

As far as music, we believe that the material you are working on will do fine. The only suggestions we might make would be for more study of theory to better understand the technical tie-in of musical vibrations to the DNA in each person. As far as actually playing, any of the classics will be good. We would like to encourage you to work on your own compositions for a short time each day, not just in practicing the performance of them, but to compose additional pieces and finish those started.

We like your thoughts on learning the music of Couperin as this was one of your previous incarnations. It would lend itself to helping people believe in reincarnation if you were to perform music you wrote in a former life and then music you have written in this life. This would open many minds as to the validity of drawing on former knowledge for use in the present incarnation.

Yes, please keep in mind what was given as far as the C chord and hearing it as a connection. It takes you right to the musical universe if you want to go there. This is where we are now to give the updates on the Science of

Music. You will need to have other images to access correctly other parts of the channel. You should have an entrance code to each different aspect of the channel you want to reach, similar to the access code for your computer. Let the C major chord be your access to the Musical Universe. For the Abdo Council you might try a visual code such as a picture of a conference table filled with the Board of Directors and settle your image on whoever is at the head of the table. For Donoray you might want to picture a door opening between two rooms of the same house as a simple entrance to this section. On the front of this door is a sign saying Science. Incidentally the more you practice this in any location or experience, the better you will be able to reach deeper streams of thought. For instance, when working at any of your jobs involving music, simply tune yourself with the C major chord and we will be there closer to the surface of your mind with innovative ideas. The same with non-scientific discussions you have with other people – see the conference table and when discussing any aspect or even thinking about any aspect of the scientific projects picture opening the door to the room marked science. As far as sitting or standing, it will not matter, once you learn to access different aspects of the channel by their separate codes. Your material is showing the goal of perfection and this is what you chose to do, not only show the goal but enable these goals to be implemented on the earth plane.

Yes, we are here, not as many of us as usual due to other events that are needing to have our attention, but at least one of us, and most of the time more, is available to you at all times. We are not exactly seated around a large conference table as you are picturing, but this does seem to help the connection. Also use the C chord along with the picture of us and we will be even more tightly connected. You see, we are permanent residents in your mind. This takes place as a matter of personal growth. We can never be separated from you and you cannot be from us. Even if you would wish to be, you cannot be separated from us. We are melded together. You are part of the Abdo Council on the earth plane and this is a very important part of the council. You see, we could sit up here at our conference table and issue decrees and send out thoughts etc. forever, but without the anchor on the earth plane it would all be for nothing. This is the way it has been for all the centuries that man has inhabited the earth until now – without the anchor on earth, or very few anchors on earth. The tremendous breakthroughs in inter-dimensional communication have been so rapid and so great that it is very difficult for humanity to keep up with the changes that we would like to see take place, now that we finally can get our thoughts and ideas to those on earth. This is causing breakdowns in the mental and physical equipment of humans and will continue to cause breakdowns unless humanity continues to raise their consciousness. Once this communication breakthrough has taken place there is no way it can be reversed, nor should it be reversed. This is the law of the universe.

Overcoming Blockages

We are here as always just under the surface. There is movement taking place within you that is good. You are dissipating blockages but it will take much more concentrated effort on your part by finding a focus for your attention. To try to overcome blockages with nothing to take their place is impossible. Even if you replace your

focus on your blockages with your music it will help, but
your focus on blockages should be replaced with a healthy
focus on yourself. We realize you are trying to do that and
it is very difficult for you because this was not the way you
were brought up or the way you have lived your life up
until now. But it is the correct way.

The thing you need to do is focus on being present in
the moment. This is difficult for one who sees the overview
and always needs to have a goal to work towards. You have
a goal, you have many goals and that is part of the problem.
Why not narrow them down, simplify them and simplify
your life and work slowly towards fulfilling your goals. If
one of these goals is realized it starts a boomerang effect
and another will follow and another, but action is the key
to it. Do not be afraid to take action. Sometimes taking
action is all that is needed to overcome blocks such as you
are facing. We deem it wise to take action on finding
another place to live. This has served you well but it is time
to move and get away from the old vibrations that are
found here. Wipe the slate clean.

Your true mastership is the creation of the perfect
human being. This is why you are going through the
struggles. You cannot reach your knowledge of the perfect
way for a human to develop if you do not go through the
pathway towards it. Miss Eva (who brought through the
Pathwork material) knew this and knew she had to keep
in contact with her innermost self. This is what you must
strive for. You are approaching this right now with your
channeling.

Down through the years we have tried just about every
way that can be tried to bring about more accurate
communication between planes. The way you (Norma) are

doing it has proved to be the most accurate so far. This is by thought impression. This is hard to describe. We are a thinking pin point of energy and are physically inside your brain cells at the time the channeling takes place. You might compare it to a phonograph needle going around the grooves of a record. Your own thought processes are grooving grooves at all times. We simply attach ourselves to the "needle" and put our thought impressions into the groove. When you are at rest or walking or busy with some household chore that you can do automatically, we can do this more easily. Even when you're playing music we can transfer thoughts, but when doing office work you have to concentrate on the project at hand. In other words, you are open to receive the thoughts from our "needle" most of the time anymore except when doing the office work. You, yourself know that most of your good ideas come either while doing dishes or walking. This may not be so with other channels but is for you. When you are questioned about a certain subject the thought will be there in your mind and will flash up as a thought initially. As soon as the thought comes, a mental image is formed automatically.

This will explain why some things are not expressed in more detail. If you write the thought down as it first flashes up it is incomplete. Thoughts that have more time to "center in" by working through the mental visualization will be more complete. A mental image is not like seeing a vision. It is still more in the thought processes than in any external area of the brain, which is where visions on any dimension take place, even earth plane vision. This then, this mental thought picture must filter out to the outside visionary functions and this is where it loses detail – in the filtering process. We know of no way to improve this except perhaps you, as you channel, can be trained to be more observant of detail in the mental thought stage, by drawing or doing oil painting.

Channeling Similar to a Telephone Message or a Fax

At different times I was told that the use of the channel was like using a telephone. That it would be the same for them as it is for us when our phone rings. They answer the call and are included for a short time in our world, in our existence. Then the connection is broken and they go about their business, the same as we do after hanging up from a phone call.

Then I was told that the information would begin coming as a "fax" that I received at night. I had felt several of these as flashes of light just as I was dropping off to sleep. They quite often startled me. I asked about them. This was at one of the times when I was trying to get an experiment going to prove the concept of the solar project.

The following excerpts are from some of the different channeling sessions that I've done recently. Excerpts have been chosen that further explain channeling:

#1 - Yes, we have been waiting. You did, indeed, receive a "fax" last night. You can now tell when this happens and need to be sure to respond with a channeling session. You will also find that they will be sent in response to your inquires and also at random. If there is something specific you wish to ask, you will receive the information. On the other hand, when we feel there is something that needs to be sent we will do so. And now we will proceed to bring through the information requested. It is from the Musical Universe but was given to them by one higher who sent it down for interpretation through musical understanding because of the tuning of the mirror for the solar project. This one is established on the tenth plane of experiment in this universe and also is in touch with the experimental divisions of three other planets. We want to have clear understanding on this test so the project can get off the ground.

#2 - As far as your concern about channels dying horrible deaths; this was part of their life plan, as something they needed to experience. You cannot ever judge another for the way he/she lives their lives or chooses to leave the earth plane. This is far too personal a choice and decisions like this are made before entry. Miss Roberts (Jane Roberts, channel for the Seth material) chose to experience this after her assigned work was done because she determined she needed to experience this sort of crossing in order to be able to help with this situation in the next life when she returns. She did indeed progress her soul greatly by this past incarnation and will soon return to further the work she began this past lifetime. She wants you to know that she is fine, that she did indeed want to experience this and will use the experience to help others even before she incarnates again.

Powerful Being Inside

I have several questions. One of them relates to the statement made that "we need to bring up our undesirable attitudes and bring them into the light and let them expand or transmute into good attitudes" and also that "our greatest weaknesses will become our greatest strengths."

I also need to know what exactly it is that I need to do to reach a deeper part of my own beingness. I feel that I'm still only in touch with the surface of me.

- What will I find there?
- How will I know when I've contacted it?
- Have I ever contacted it?
- Is there really any more to me than I already know?
- If so, would it survive in the real world if I let it grow and expand in real life?
- What kind of a person would that make me?
- Why am I scared to continue with finding me?
- Is there anything I can do to hasten my transmutation?
- How should I utilize the sessions with the Pathwork teacher? I want to take full advantage of this opportunity because of the expense and the long drive to get to the Pathwork sessions. I really want to cooperate.
- If I take it on myself to eliminate a bad attitude of jealousy, for instance, what would happen if I let it expand and grow?
- What would it transmute into? I can't imagine how this weakness could be turned into a great strength.

Please freeflow about all of this and touch on as much of it as you can to help me understand. Thank you.

I suddenly feel different – very confident and self-assured. I didn't consciously call in the channel but it seems to be here. This is different. Please explain.

Yes, you are the channel now. You will have to work even harder than before to establish it again to the point where it was before. But it will be the correct way to channel. Just relax and let your own mind bring to you the answers to the questions you have asked. This mind, your own mind really is the real you. You have been in touch with it before but in a relay situation whereas it was being translated to you by a being from another planet who would look inside your soul and read and interpret what was there. This will no longer be taking place. You are truly on your own now. You will look and interpret your own soul. Your soul is ready to begin if you are.

Your question about transmuting attitudes is what we would like to bring through first. By the use of the word "we" you are designating the combined you and your soul. Keep your own mind focused into this channeling session. Be very aware and alert as to what is being said. Know that it is coming from your deeper, innermost beingness. This is why you feel the confidence right now. You are connected for the time being.

I have more questions.

- What was that incredibly large, beautiful expansion that I've experienced twice now?
- Is this what I'm looking for?
- Was that the real me?
- If so, how could anything that powerful function on the earth plane? It would be an impossible situation.
- How, then, can a person let this part of themselves out and incorporate it into the real world?
- Is this what we should do or should it truly just be there for our times of communion with our inner God? Please elaborate on this and why it happened.

- Should I try to let it happen again?
- Should I try to hold it and keep it with me at all times? Please help.

Yes, that was you, the real you. It was quite magnificent. This is not your channel now. I am a member of the Abdo group. That magnificence is what we see when we tune into your beingness. We do not see the petty little child that is pouting on the earth plane because she is not getting her way. We see this fantastic, overpowering, beautiful being and feel compassion because of what it has to try and work with and express through as far as you on the earth plane. No human could contain the power and magnificence of this being that is really you. Do you remember when you played that song in church and the energy came through so strong you were shaking and lost your voice for two weeks? It was this part of your being that came through. The power was too great and it backed off. It was this part of you that came through at the concert in Fort Collins when people in the audience saw an eight foot tall figure overshadowing you. That is what you recently contacted. You have a whole lot of growing and expanding to do for this being to ever be able to express through you on the earth. It has never had a physical form that it could express through due to the power behind it. It realizes this and therefore does not push its way to the front in any of your lifetimes or we should say in any of its lifetimes. It is not an impossible task, but you would surely be considered a saint of some kind if it managed to come through you. Vocal channeling would help open and expand the physical vessel for this expression to happen, but you are afraid to vocal channel because of the power behind it.

What can we say? You have the power to decide on whether you want to let this incredible part of you out into the world to do all the good you could accomplish or whether you wish to cause this part of you to be continually frustrated. We would like to encourage you to let it out into the world. The feeling of ecstasy you would live in would at all times surpass any feeling you would get of physical satisfaction with another human being. You would live in total ecstasy while performing the most enormous good deeds for your brother man. Please think about this and whether or not you want this part of you suppressed for all eternity.

The physical form you are in now and the circumstances of this life are so that this would be the first opportunity this part of you has ever had to come out of inner plane life and experience manifestation. You have let it out once or twice in connection with music. Music opens the door for it to come through. Remember this. Music will open the door and then the creation material and all other material will just spill through. You will not be able to stop the flow, but music is the passageway for this part of you to manifest. If you do not do your music this part of you will not attempt to come through. This seems hard for you to believe, but this part of you is music personified – the Master Musician. The worlds of musical vibration are incorporated into this part of you. Why do you think you brought the Science of Music in? It is you who has developed it from the very beginning of the universes. You know all the pathways of vibrations. Please do not shut off this channel. Just, if necessary, give it a rest. When the time is right, this part of you will be exposed to the light and your life will change so dramatically you will be amazed. This large expansive, loving, beautiful being that fills your body is the real you. How lucky you are to have experienced it. God Bless you my child.

Summary

To begin with we would like to state that the channeled material will be coming from three places, the scientific channel, the channel that can tap into the akashic records and the present time channel of synthesization for a drawing together of all information for each specific case. We are the Musical Universe. For the most part your channeling now comes from the Micro viewpoint almost exclusively except perhaps for readings and a few other instances. You are pulling from the cells of your body that are progressing towards the eighth universe, as are all cells in all bodies. When spiritual growth does not keep up, these bodies are fighting a losing battle as far as physical evolution goes. Thus disease is the outcome. The children entering need to have these truths taught to them from the moment of birth on.

I, Norma, asked for some insight on why I become embarrassed about being spiritual and being able to channel. I received the following:

When one is embarrassed it is because he is not being true to his own beliefs. Therefore, anything that you talk about with others must be that which you truly believe to be absolutely true as far as your present standing in evolution goes. Knowing that God is within you and living this truth every moment of every day, is what will aid you in overcoming your embarrassment. A sense of self-confidence and self-esteem will allow you to overcome being embarrassed. To be spiritual does not mean you have to be an "angel;" just the opposite. Some of the more truly spiritual people you meet are down to earth, very human people living their lives according to their own code of ethics, not anyone else's belief of what they should or should not do. There is no room for embarrassment when living your truth. That's what being human is all about and by being human you are being spiritual in the manner intended for your progress in that school of experience.

You need to learn to think of us as you, a part of you that you no longer wish to hide from others. This will help. You are hiding approximately 45% of your light from those who meet you. You never open the shades to let us all shine through. Knowing and admitting to yourself that there is much more of you will help. Know that almost half of your being is under the water with only 55% of the iceberg showing. Isn't this a waste of what you could do with your life? We are here within you and we are a major part of the makeup of the true you. You will never get over your embarrassment until you accept us fully and allow us to live and express through you. You cannot deny us any longer. We are integrated within you. Why not just open the door to us when you need us. This will give you self-confidence that will then allow you to not be embarrassed. We cannot force you to allow us expression, but know that most of your frustration, indecision, embarrassment, lack of confidence, depression – all the things you are going through – are caused by you denying you, the more evolved you. Why not have a "coming out party?" Know your own truth to be you and own it and own us and continue on your mission.

With your permission we will come through when it is appropriate, but you must give your permission at the beginning of each day. Greet us in the morning and give us allowance to be part of your life. If you feel frustrated think how we feel by not being allowed to be part of your life. This is what is needed. Be gentle but firm with your animal-based brain and let it know that it no longer is in control. It has its place in the scheme of things. We could not be here if it were not for the evolvement of this part of your brain, but it is time for it to allow you your full expression of the glory of your life. If not now, when?

The Musical Universe handles material from your past. The Abdo Council handles future determinations for humans. Your own channel; your personal guides and teachers which are, of course, aspects of your own personality, handles the tie-in to present day life. This is the true use of the channel and it is all to come together as one voice from an individual when the process of blending is complete. It will show the composite picture of the person bringing the channel through in this manner.

There is so much that needs to be learned and understood about channeling. There is a wealth of information in these New Millennium NoteBooks that needs to be pulled together and edited to show this picture. You are moving towards this, but very slowly. We hope that the momentum will pick up soon and that the material is made available to everyone shortly.

The ability to know these truths is inside each and everyone. Some call it the Holy Spirit, some the Divine Mind and others term it Rings of Energy. We prefer to call it the Creative Channel. Perhaps a more all-inclusive term would be Divine Inspiration.

The technical channel is coming into the stage where it works better just in your thought processes. This is a natural happening, but it does need to be documented, as you are doing, for reference, so we will continue this way. Your crown chakra is opening to the sixth level. It was opened at level four when you were born and has opened in degrees since then through level five. Now level six is opening and depending on your furtherance of channeling, level seven will not be too far behind. Level six is the incorporation of the higher thoughts into your animal-based brain. What this means is that it will seem more and more like your own mind when you are actually channeling. Even you will not be able to tell quite often that you are channeling. This is, of course, the proper way for the channel to be used. The channel is, after all, the stream of intelligence that is available to everyone who works at receiving it. The more subdued the animalistic instincts of the animal-based brain, the more strongly this stream of intelligence can enter. Therein lies the making of geniuses.

Following are some questions and answers that shed some more light on channeling for us:

Question - Benjamin Creme claims that Maitreya is in embodiment as one living in the Asian community of London. Do you agree?

Answer - This has been a rumor coming from more than just Mr. Creme. The one in England that everyone is mistaking for Maitreya is a high master, but is not Maitreya. He has entered to accomplish a mission, the subject of which we are not at liberty to discuss. The time simply is not right yet. When it is right he will let it be known.

Question - How can we distinguish between our soul's communication, our guide's communication and our inner plane teacher?

Answer - This takes much practice and trial and error. This is what the whole incarnation is all about is to learn this through experiences. The lessons or tests are always there in front of one and will be presented over and over until correct reaction is accomplished. The more blatant and insistent the voice being heard, the more probability there is that it is the personality and not that of either the soul or the teachers and guides. The soul, when giving messages, will be very soft and gently insistent, and will always leave room for free will. The messages from it will deal more in actions and reactions to circumstances in the daily life. When the realm of the inner plane teachers and guides are reached the messages will carry a more all-encompassing viewpoint, not that they won't bring personal help and guidance, but the thoughts will come on a more universal basis, such as how humanity as a whole has always responded to certain situations and isn't it time that someone, somewhere starts to change the situation.

Another way that may help distinguish which place the messages are coming from would be to liken them to different areas of your head as far as thinking goes. If you say that something is "in the back of your mind" that is probably your own soul. If something comes to you "off the top of your head" that is most likely the inner plane teachers and guides. A thought that is almost an instinctive reaction or an automatic reaction to a situation is most likely your personality. When one gets to the point where he can draw from the divine mind he will no longer need to worry about which place a message is coming from because all will be totally synthesized by then.

Question - Is it important to have knowledge of the distinction between those two?

Answer - Yes it is important to have knowledge of the distinction because this is wherein the progress of the incarnation lies. The more ability one has to distinguish between messages, the faster his progress will be.

Question - Can we receive direct communication from God as opposed to our soul and guides, etc.?

Answer - Only when a certain level of growth is attained. It is not so much that God speaks to you as it is that you contact the thoughts of the Creator. Most people think they are hearing the voice of God when it could be any one of the other places we receive messages from. Usually when one is communicating directly with God they are not going to announce it blatantly to the world because to be able to reach this point of evolvement they would no longer be interested in announcing it.

Question - Are there different levels of truth being channeled? Where are the various levels or planes? What is the causal level as it relates to the Chrysalis Teachings?

Answer - There are twelve different levels of truth and each of these levels have twelve stages within them. Therefore there are at least 144 different levels of truth being channeled at any one time by all the various channels who will all color them because they come through the personality of that channel. Learning to discriminate between them is one of the many lessons for humanity at this stage of evolution. Your decision to trust in any one particular channel shows us the level of your involvement. The various levels and planes are described in Volume II of Truths of Man's Divine Heritage by Norma. The causal plane referred to in other material is the combined levels of 4-5-6 in the Chrysalis Teachings.

Question - Typically, some channels pay attention to spiritual evolvement and encouraging humanity to not feel guilt and fear. The Chrysalis material is very scientific. Is there any reason for the priority that is being given to scientific material over spiritual material in the Chrysalis Teachings? Please clarify and explain.

Answer - Those working with the spirituality of individuals are working from a lower plane or dimension.

When you are at the level the Chrysalis Teachings are coming from you are spiritual. You do not need to have the instruction and the outward display that those not as evolved need to have. This would also apply to the channel that is chosen to be used. The channel must also be of higher evolution. Being spiritual means nothing more than being the best person you can as far as your interaction with your brothers and sisters and doing what you are capable of to help all of humanity. Science is spiritual. The two are interrelated to the point where they cannot be separated. To be one is to be the other. Your Creator is scientifically perfect. What other way could a human be? To be as perfect as his Creator he must be scientific. Those working on individual concepts of personal spirituality are working in the lower right division, the emotional body. They will progress in each life towards the higher concepts until they too reach a point of knowing that science and spirituality cannot be separated.

Question - Can you comment on The Course of Miracles? Who channeled it and what level or dimension were they at?

Answer - The Course in Miracles was channeled on the other side by Jesus Sananda (His universal name) Himself. At that time He was above the twelfth dimension in the outer limits of our solar system. It was one of the beginning messages to begin the plan of awareness for humanity that is still ongoing. The Course in Miracles was an early attempt to bring humanity out of the "guilt trip" that the churches had put them on. It was to enlighten them as to the fact that each individual has equal worth in the eyes of the Creator, that all are on an individual path and that none should judge another. These are excellent teachings and are still valid today because beginning seekers still need to have this knowledge. They must have this background in order to be able to accept the Chrysalis Teachings. The two courses would compliment each other.

Question - Are there any dangers involved with channeling? If so, what are they and how can one protect oneself from them?

Answer - There are dangers involved with the beginning stages of channeling. Most of these dangers come from the person's own make-up. It involves their duality. There is some danger from the astral plane, but if one is channeling due to a natural opening of the channel this will not be as big a problem as it will be if one has forced the channel open. Also, the first lifetime when the channel opens is the one in which most danger will be apparent. If one has channeled in other lives, then his use of the channel is well established and he automatically overcomes the problems.

As stated, the biggest danger is generated from within the being of the one learning to channel for the first time. He must be in close touch with either an earth plane teacher or the inner plane guides. The inner plane guides become confused in his mind with the entities wanting to come through the channel. These will be, in the beginning, the past lives of the one learning to channel. If they had a devious one in their past, and for some reason this one was either allowed to come through to clear up something, or was chosen to be an influence on this life for some other quality he had, then this one could want to take over. He would even imitate the inner plane guides if necessary to allow the personality on the earth to let him come through. This is wherein the danger lies.

At this stage, the type of information coming through must be assessed very intelligently. If it is glorifying to the channel then question it. It is all right if it deals with personal matters in the beginning if the material coming through deals with common sense advice and logical approaches to problems. But if any of it suggests an act or deed that the channel himself would not contemplate doing in his daily life, then question this material closely; question who is bringing it through and why. Have them state their purpose and be very firm about what you will do to help them and what you won't. Inform them that their turn will come to clear up unfinished business, but it is your life and you determined to only work on certain aspects of your karma. If the karma carried with you this time was not caused by their deeds in a previous life, then they must await the next personality to be spun from the same seedcore for their karma to be cleared, if even then. It may be possible that their karma will not be cleared in a personal manner. It may be put off until having to be cleared in a general karmic matter. If they had no good points to their life that can be incorporated into the whole, then that particular personality will not have any part of him become part of the seedcore that lives eternal life. This is important and this entity will be one that will panic and try to lead and take over the one on the earth plane. This is one example of possession and one of the hardest to deal with.

Question - Can you tell me what part breath and breath control play as far as channeling?

Answer - The part that breath and breath control play, as far as an individual's evolution, is that of a facilitator for reaching the higher realms in a meditative state. Naturally breath and breathing is very important to the functioning of the physical body, but this is not what your question is about. Breath and breathing have not been stressed in the Chrysalis Teachings partly due to the fact that the channel never used this facilitating method, and partly because the material coming through this channel has never stressed individual development. Her role is not in that arena. She has experienced a little of the breath and the breath control and realizes there is a validity to it, but in her particular case it was not necessary. In other particular cases it may not be necessary either. Each one is an individual. If one has good experiences by using breath and breath control, then certainly you should use it. But to not use it is not going to stop the development. It is most definitely used in vocal singing and therefore would be of much help in the vocal channeling area. This would enable a channel to be able to develop the necessary endurance for longer periods of vocal channeling.

Question - Astrology tells us that during those periods when the planet Mercury is in retrograde, that communications between people tend to be quite difficult and there is often a great deal of misunderstanding. Similarly, contracts and agreements made during these periods often fail or are broken by either or both parties. Is it possible that channeling could also be affected? In other words, is there a greater potential for misunderstanding of channeled material when the planet Mercury is in retrograde?

Answer - There is a definite effect on channeling by astrological events. It has much to do with the astrological signs that a particular channel is born under, but will affect all channels to one degree or another. The power and influence of certain events cause the channel to bring through the information colored by the influence of certain planets that are in line with the earth at that particular time, combined with the channels own astrological influences. There are so many variables that can affect channeling that it is a wonder that any of it reaches the earth plane in any degree of accuracy.

For the most part, the earth plane channel has the most effect on the material. The astrological influences are to the interpretation the channel puts on the material. It does not come from any astrological influence on the material itself. In the case of this particular channel there is very little influence from Mercury being in retrograde as far as how she is interpreting the material. It is having an effect on her ability to clearly and precisely draw it to her, but not on her interpretation. In other words, Mercury being in retrograde is affecting her exoterically, not esoterically. Her own astrological signs are such at this time that they counter any negative influences that Mercury might have on interpretation, but there is one aspect of her chart that is allowing a physical reaction to the present astrological influences of Mercury.

Question - In Jon Klimo's book "Channeling" on page 224 it states: In hypnotically induced experiences, researchers cannot agree on whether the entity is the actual historical past-life persona of the hypnotized subject, or a channeled being separate from the subject and her past lives, or a sub-personality of the subject's dissociated unconscious mind. Careful content analysis of the information communicated in these situations is often the only way to begin to resolve the matter. To date, the method leaves much open to interpretation. Could you please comment on this?

Answer - The answer to this puzzling problem is that is a combination of the past life of the spiritual entity residing in that body and a genetically carried memory passed through the physical body. When a person is hypnotized by another it will never be a channeled entity of a separate makeup from the unmanifested state, because they do not come through hypnotically induced trances (trances induced by someone outside the form being hypnotized). They cannot get through the paralyzing action that is caused to the brain cells in this sort of a hypnotic trance. This type of hypnosis is not the proper way to help people. It quite often causes a problem in that some of the brain cells never do return to their full function. They remain inactive, or still in a trance, even after most of the rest of the brain has come back out of the trance. When a trance is self-induced this does not take place. It is the effect of the energy of the hypnotist not blending in harmony with the energy of the subject being hypnotized. In a self-induced trance this disharmony is not there and there is no permanent blocking of movement from these cells which makes it easier for entities other than those coming from the subject's own being to come through.

Chapter 11

THE SPACE SHIP PHENOMENA

"I really love this picture you took of my cat Clemmie on the bed," I said to Neil. "Sometimes I'd watch her sleeping and see her paws move like she was running and I'd wonder what she was dreaming about."

My cat, Clemmie

"I guess I never thought much about animals dreaming." Neil answered. "Do you think they do?"

"I really don't know. The TimeTraveler tried to explain to me what happens when you go to sleep and he talked about animals, but it was kind of complicated. Would you like to read it and see if you understand?" I asked.

"Sure, I'm up for it. Let's do it," he replied.

Duality

Everything in the universe is of a dual nature, a dual make-up. This includes all kingdoms. This duality is the make-up of two different atomic substances. One is of matter and form, the other is of ether and thought. We are familiar with thought-forms and ethereal-matter. Ethereal-matter is what holds and contains the thought-forms. Now we would like to discuss matter-form and ethereal-thought.

Matter-form is of lower vibratory frequency; ethereal-thought is of higher vibratory rate. One would be considered to consist of sub-atomic particles and the other to consist of ventrete atomic particles, which simply means of infinitesimal size. The central core of all universes is this ventrete atomic matter. The word ventrete word implies expansion. Perhaps this will help explain micro men and spaceships. It is a controllable thing, but is influenced by many factors.

Being a Micro Man

I am a micro man. I am very, very, tiny; as tiny as you when you are on the inner planes at night. Remember, your animal brain is asleep. It is of matter-form. Your divine spark never sleeps. It is of ethereal-thought. When you are on the inner planes you are in ethereal-form and matter-thought is not present. Do you see the reversal that takes place? On the inner planes you have the divine spark in ethereal-form, and in your bed, you have the animal brain in matter-thought. This can help explain differences in dreams and why they are so hard to interpret.

At times the matter-thought is dreaming. This is at the sub-levels of sleep. Yes, this part of you will dream just as also dogs, cats, and other animals dream. It will be dreams of your exoteric life, and have materialistic connotations having to do with things pertaining to your physical body. For instance, cats will dream of chasing mice and their paws will even reenact running. So also your animal brain will dream in matter-thought.

Your ethereal form cannot leave; it cannot pull out of the matter-thought until this sub-level of dreams is finished and the animal brain totally at rest. Then the higher vibrations can begin to build and the ethereal-form can rise. When we say rise, we do not mean literally rise off the bed. We mean rise up through the layers of the matter-thought that surrounds it and be a free-form energy, then, to do as it pleases. This is when you actually also become a micro man. The ethereal-form is smaller with smaller wave patterns and tinier atomic particles – micro, in other words. You are composed of both. We are composed of both, only our natural state is the complete reversal of yours. We are at all times in ethereal-form, not matter-thought. We are thought-forms in ethereal-matter. You are matter-thought not in ethereal-forms.

Together on the Inner Planes

When you are on the inner planes at night and become micro, we are together in either study or relaxation. When you cannot come to us due to the heavy matter-form of your animal brain, then neither can we come to you. As many different ways as there are to see us and contact us, so it is

211

with our vehicles and animal-powered transportation, and remember, the choice is always yours. We cannot come through matter-forms that have no ethereal-thought blended into them. This is why some can see us and some can't, and the higher a person's vibratory rate is does not increase his chance of seeing us, because if he really wants to he can see the lower forms. If he really wants to he can also see the higher forms. The choice is his.

Now when he makes this choice to want to see us is when our time of making a choice to be seen comes into play. Sometimes we do choose to be seen and cannot be due to many factors that influence the event. These would be atmospheric conditions, motives of those wanting to see us, vibratory rate of locale on earth, etc. In the early life of planet earth it was easier to cross mind dimension & planets due to the state the earth herself was in – a molten pliable form. The more it hardens, so does matter-form harden and make it more difficult for ethereal-thought to enter.

Norma's First Experience in a Micro Body

The first time I experienced this I was told: The feeling you had the night before when you were working all night on the newsletter (while in bed sleeping) was that of all-encompassing, all-pervading of self into matter. This is difficult. You were experiencing being a micro man, which is in essence what devas are.

You see, each individual spark is so tiny, so infinitesimal, that it is no bigger than a pin-head in each body. It was not the spark that couldn't enter the deva (an entity without a soul), it was the soul. The soul is what weights five ounces. The spark is that of a minute bit of

212

electrical energy that is as a radioactive or nuclear reactor in each human body. This spark, this divine spark can and does enter devas. It is the soul – where the conscience is formed – that cannot enter the deva. This needs to be understood.

As one of these micro-men, you can experience and did experience being one with your publications. This is that feeling of being every part of it – the paper, the type, the picture, the whole product, one period or comma. At the same time you are a part of all the "matter" essentials. You are also the "total" gist of subject matter taking form in the matter world. In other words you are the Creator God of your publications. This is an exact analogy of God in His world that He created. As you could experience, through your creativity, the feeling of being a comma or that of a question mark or that of a bold face lettering or an underlined word that helps with expressing your thoughts-forms, so is it with God in His micro-man ability to pervade all and experience all.

Now were God to pull His feelings out and not express and feel through each of you and all things of all kingdoms, (compare to paper, type, color, weight, etc.) there would be no spark, no vibration of electrical energy in the whole world. People would be as robots or clones or inanimate kingdoms such as a rock without a feel and look and glow, or a plant that was limp and dull, or a bird that couldn't fly or sing, or a human that couldn't express beauty and joy. What kind of a world would there be without God, the divine spark of electricity that pervades and experiences all?

As you can sense disharmony in a misspelled word or an incomplete sentence in your creation of books and newsletters, so can God sense disharmony in some part of

His creation. As you will change or delete a misspelled word or add to and finish an incomplete sentence in your creations, so will God in His creation.

What you were experiencing was the totality of that blending into wholeness that we experience here on the twelfth plane before we exit. The lecture you received last night was from planet twelve. It concerned the futility of many lives that humans drift through. If they but realized the consequences of lack of purpose, they would immediately change the direction of their path. The lives are numbered twelve for each twelve tones of the scale. If one is wasted this tone never becomes a full-bodied "perfect pitch" and will always be the one tone that will not blend harmonically with others.

Norma's Second Experience in a Micro Body

The second time I experienced being a micro man happened again at night while in bed sleeping. I woke from a dream in the middle of the night and described to the guides the next morning what I remembered of that dream. This was the feeling of being a whole brain, just a thought-form, inside a human body, correcting something that was not right in that body. It also seemed as though the person whose body it was, was also in there with me. I believe it was a female form and that we were working on the reproductive organs, as I remember seeing a row of eggs sitting there waiting. I asked the guides if they could please interpret, or help me interpret this?

I received the following: Yes, we can and will. This is the area that your training on the inner planes is in now – healing humanity's' bodies physically, emotionally, and mentally leading them to the spiritual.

214

You were most definitely in spiritual form. It is well that we woke you when this feeling was total within you, as this is the only way we have of explaining ourselves to you. It was I who was in there with you, it was not the person the body belonged to. I am training you at night in this subject, yes, through the orders of David. That is all we will say. You know I am not him, but it is through his orders. His name will be as a password for your peace of mind. Do you understand?

You were working on the ovaries of one whom you do know and are in close contact with, as there is a slight problem in this area. We did not need to have her permission on the physical plane as you have it on the inner planes. This is the process known on your plane as menopause that this one is going through. The menses had not totally stopped due to one slight imperfection in the form in this area and as you recall, all it took was one little snip to uncurl the tube and let nature, which is God in the inner body form, take its course. In this one, the hormone balance is doing its job, the physical body was not. The consequences could have been serious, but we did foresee this and have taken these steps to help this one and also to train you.

We will be doing more of this in the future. You did the actual snipping, as you remember. And yes, you're thinking, it is as though you held scissors in your hand when you did it, but on the other hand you remember yourself as one big round blob. Is this not true? Able to do anything that the human form can do without having that human form because it is as a thought-form that you snipped this piece of flesh. And it as a thought-form that this piece of flesh received that snip. And as thoughts are things, it became a reality the moment you performed the task. This feeling that you awoke remembering is pervasion, one aspect of pervasion that we were discussing, the totality aspect of pervasion that was your total ability to enter into this body and perform the necessary task.

Micro Men Are In Space Ships

The guides and teachers live in space/time, you live in time/space. We exist in a space on the map of the carpet of time. You exist in a time that has a place in space. The teachers and guides exist eternally without any time constraints, which is why the universe is endless. Humans live in a time capsule which exists only at a certain small spot on the map. You do not expand into space and have it endless as we do because of the constraints of time. It is as though you are clothed in an outer layer of clothing that holds you in place. We do not have this constraint. We live in space, you live in time.

Our purpose on the earth plane is as it always was, to help our brethren understand their far reaching universe. It all has to do with macro and micro perceptions. There is no way you can experience what you consider the large universe in the reality that you display on the earth plane. The only way it can ever be understood and explained is through the use of the "power converter," that steps the universe down to your dimension. You can experience and know and understand all through your inner vision.

The very ones who condemn psychic power are the ones we need to reach. Thus our problem. They will be reached however, one by one if necessary. This will take a long time on your plane, therefore we are intervening to speed this up. We can reach them one by one much more quickly than anyone in manifestation can reach them. The "job" or "task," if you will, of those on the earth plane who are enlightened and are dedicated to helping us is to be available to follow up with the teaching of those individuals as we awaken them.

We Need to Work in Cooperation with Micro Men

If we work in cooperation the process of bringing earth up in vibratory frequency will be much speeded up. This is our purpose for coming to your earth plane, as once your vibratory rate increases, so many wonderful spiritual happenings will be available that wars will stop overnight and all on earth will "feel" the love and blessings of their Creator. All things false will be eliminated. This will prevent the things that are being uncovered in the churches at the present time from happening again. These episodes are not over yet and are a necessary prelude to peace. We are sickened by what we see taking place and it is well that most do not see what is happening to their hard earned money they so trustingly donate to these "ill" ministers of television and radio. These sick ministers will be paying karma to humanity for a long, long time if allowed at all to stay in the realm of the earth dimension. They certainly are not serving God, only themselves and must be considered very dangerous as they are endangering the spiritual bodies of mankind, not just the physical bodies.

This is why we are here, to help raise the vibration of mankind into harmony with the higher planes. A discord in music can make some ill and this is what earth is causing, a discord in the harmony of the spheres. When received in love from you on earth, there is no cause for alarm or fear. If we are met with violence, we will respond in violence. The time draws ever nearer.

We believe that people are now ready to accept the scientific reality of what UFO experiences are. To begin with, a UFO experience precedes the "Rebirth into Continuity" that has been discussed before.

This rebirth takes place due to, or because of, the UFO experience. How soon or how long after the UFO experience this rebirth takes place depends on the person's acceptance within his soul of what he saw and experienced. If he believes it deep within himself, regardless of what others around him think, then his rebirth will come soon after that. If he, himself, has doubts and listens to other's opinions and buries the experience, then the rebirth will come much later or not at all in this lifetime.

UFO Sightings Similar to a Hologram

The sensation of seeing, really seeing the UFO or the alien entity is truly similar to a hologram. It is a vibratory picture from another dimension that is focused into and superimposed on the reality picture a person sees of the third dimension. The same effect or a similar effect could be manifested on the earth with a hologram. We have stated in the past that those working on scientific projects would understand them much better if they studied holograms. We suggest the same thing for UFO researchers.

The UFO contactee is one of the person's own former incarnations or personalities. The seedcore is responsible for determining which former personality is sent on this mission. It normally chooses one that is sympathetic with what the person living on the earth plane is all about. The contactee, or "alien," will be similar in interests and goals and perhaps used the same strengths in his own previous incarnation, so is very close in make up to the one on earth. This helps with the contact because of the "like attracts like" principle which acts as a magnet.

Group Sightings Are Seedcore Families

Since the whole experience takes place inside the mind or minds of those experiencing it, each one of them will retain the memory of it differently – each according to his own personal reality background which consists of all he has ever been since the beginning of time. This explains the fact that several people seeing the same UFO will have different impressions of it afterwards to relate to others. These different impressions that each person gives after a sighting should be thoroughly studied because herein lies some of the secrets of beingness for this particular person. It will point the person toward his main goal in this life by the subject matter of the impressions he receives when having a UFO experience.

The reason many people see them at one time is due to the fact of seedcore groupings on the earth plane. You realize, of course, that families, seedcore families, reincarnate into human families for the first six lives of the twelve lives spent in third dimensional consciousness. The ones on the sixth life are the ones who will have these experiences because this is the breakthrough into the next six lives which do not have to return into incarnation as a family member working on personal issues. They have "graduated" if you will from this type of reincarnation and can now come back as upper level classroom members working on seedcore projects. You can readily see that this is really is a big spiritual event in the life of a person.

Some people have these experiences while asleep and if they are not in the habit of consciously remembering their dreams, they will not know of the event and will therefore not recognize the "Rebirth into Continuity" when it takes place.

Inner and Outer Spacemen

There are certain entities outside the human realm that do not have emotional bodies. These are from lower evolved universes and are the ones we have spoken about as being those in the spaceships that are seen with the physical eyes. They are the outer spacemen instead of the inner spacemen. We have warned that contact with them cannot further your spiritual growth. It can enhance your exoteric knowledge of the universe and other planets, but contact with them will never be the way to attain spiritual growth. They are interested in humanity from a selfish point of view, only to further their own knowledge.

The inner spacemen, on the other hand, are those who have evolved through earth plane evolutionary processes both manifested and unmanifested. These are the ones that Norma has been in contact with from the beginning. She has never in been in contact with the other kind. We guarded her against this happening. She has printed warnings we have sent through in the newsletter about the other kind, but for the most part humanity does not understand that there are two different kinds of space people and different kinds of spaceships. The kinds of spaceships are of a wider variety for the outer spacemen than our spaceships. Our spaceships are only seen through the single eye unless a special occasion warrants otherwise.

Many humans get in trouble by their fascination with the spaceships they see with their eyes. This would not be so dangerous if they had previously had contact with the inner spacemen and knew the difference, but this is not usually the case. Humans need to be educated about the true facts of UFOs and guarded against listening to the space people who are emotionless. In fact, your emotional body is one of the big attractions your planet has for them. They are envious of your ability to feel.

The inner spacemen, have polished their emotional body to the point where it is smooth and even and transmuted into unconditional love. Therefore, you could technically say we no longer have an emotional body, but we did have and have spent eternity working with it to bring it into spiritual understanding. This does become easier when the twin souls are blended once again and the entity feels more whole within himself. This takes place on levels of blending. The first level is just within each incarnation. Then there is a blending when earth plane incarnations are ended, then there is a further blending when joining the oversoul.

Chapter 12

UFOS FROM OUTSIDE OUR SOLAR SYSTEM

"Where did you get this picture of space ships?" Neil asked as we continued looking through the pictures on my computer.

"I kind of cheated for that one. I scanned in an illustration from a book and then made several different sizes and tilted them different ways," I replied. "I thought it was pretty clever and usable to illustrate some things the TimeTraveler talked about," I continued.

"It is pretty realistic looking," Neil said

"Let's tune into the TimeTraveler and hear what he was talking about as far as space ships," I said.

"Okay with me," Neil replied.

UFOs From Outside Our Solar System

The type of UFO that is from outside your solar system can be seen by anyone who has already experienced his rebirth into continuity, either in this life or in a past life, if this person is truly open to other dimensions in this life. This is also a personal choice depending on what it is this person wished to accomplish as goals in this life. If he chose a goal to review some elementary attitudes, he would not have chosen to be open to other dimensions as this would deter him from his goal. Being a graduated being that is working for the seedcore this quite often happens because it takes one of higher evolutionary standing to be able to handle a lifetime of regression, which is what this is for him. This is why we should never judge anyone for the experiences he is having in this lifetime. The more deplorable his life is, the more you must be sure that he is a highly evolved being working in a time warp situation to progress the growth and evolvement of his seedcore family. He should not be judged. His own soul knows what it is he is here for. This is the only judge he should have – his own soul.

UFO Experience is Breaking of Membrane in Brain

To return to our discussion of the hologram scene, this is caused by the separation of the veil or membrane that exists between the first section of the brain and the second section. There are thinner membranes between the twelve levels in each section and some people do recognize these when they are torn away, but most don't. In some cases they will be felt as severe pains shooting through the head. In others they will be a rather worse than usual headache. In some dizziness will be the effect of the breaking of these smaller membranes. But there is only once that the effect will be felt and experienced as a UFO experience and it is when one passes into the second section of the brain. This is a great spiritual experience and should be celebrated internally by the one who has the UFO experience.

People need to be educated about this. Evolution is going to continue whether or not people want to look at these things. They are holding back the rest of the citizens of their particular solar system and even the whole universe when they choose to bury their head in the sand and not keep up with the known facts of their evolutionary progress. This is considered a crime against universal law because, as it's been stated in the past, it is wrong to hold others back in their spiritual progress.

Sightings Similar to Seeing Rainbows

A hologram is difficult to describe to one with no knowledge along these lines. It is made up of bits and pieces of film, to use an analogy. These bits and pieces of film are floating free in the atmosphere actually in chaos. For one brief instant in time the person on the earth plane acts as a magnet that pulls them together in perfect sequence to manifest as a real object. A rainbow is a very good comparison to what we are talking about. You can see the rainbow, take a picture of it but you cannot ever catch it or touch it. Depending on the circumstances of the atmospherical conditions that caused the rainbows appearance, you can also feel – as an electrical sensation – the effect of the rainbow in the atmosphere. This is exactly the same thing that takes place when an person has a vision on the earth plane or sees their teacher or guide as a real, living person on the earth plane. This is actually an advanced state of the same process as seeing a UFO.

This ability is inborn within all. Everyone is born having the ability to see rainbows. This lasts until the spiritual experience of rebirth that of seeing a UFO, takes place. A more in depth use of this ability to see rainbows or UFOs is the ability to see the teachers and guides – beings from another dimension – and then, finally, after many lifetimes of using these abilities, they are able to see visions – real action taking place on the earth plane from another dimension. This formerly was called having second sight. Your grandmother, Miss Norma, had this ability. Some people experience this as looking at past events that for some reason they need to review in this life. These are mini time warps. Others experience these as looking into the future. It all depends on the person and his past, and also the goal of his present incarnation.

We hope this has helped some people understand what has happened to them. We hope it will help acceptance be gained for this business of UFO sightings. We hope this will help eliminate the fear that these sightings bring. We hope it will give hope to our beautiful brothers and sisters on the earth plane, who truly do not understand. We sincerely hope that this discourse stretches and opens minds that are closed to the very subject that could literally change their life forever – a great leap forward in spiritual growth. So be it.

The Greek Oracles

The Greek oracles were actually those who had come down in space ships to help humanity. They were not channels as you know them now. There were many who dedicated their existence to filling the position of oracles. They kept themselves hidden for several reasons. They did not want to mix with humanity because of the difference in vibration and also because they felt the people would accept the advise given if they thought it was coming was God. It was not wrong of them to do this because they were from God the same as all are from God.

One Woman's Personal Experience

When asked to explain the experience a friend went through several years ago we received the following explanation: Your friend went into another dimension of time. Her physical body continued to operate on the third level which is still part of the animal brain system. The higher self was taken to level seven where it received many spiritual truths in that hour and a half time period. The little light was a micro man aura that guided her on her travels. He did leave a guide in the car with her, also a micro man.

This is how we were able to operate at that time. Things have moved swiftly and we are able to accomplish much of the teaching in a direct feed into the higher mind levels, sometimes at night and sometimes while the entity is busy doing tasks that require only subconscious activity. She was allowed to see herself talking to the neighbor so the incident would come into her memory system and induce her to begin her spiritual search. If she had not seen herself, she would have been frightened afterwards thinking she had amnesia. This is what most temporary cases of amnesia are.

This explanation should reassure her that she is on the right path for her at last. This was the purpose behind the incident. We are glad to be able to enlighten her and encourage her to search deeply for those lessons given her at that time. This is why the books she has read all have meaning to her. She knows internally that they speak the truth, as she experienced the same truths that day.

This was an excursion aboard a space ship, by the way. The micro man escorted her spirit mind aboard the ship where she attended several lectures and also a private session with a group of teachers and guides. This will all start coming back to her as she meditates on the incident. She will eventually be able to draw a picture of the inside of the ship.

Another Woman's Personal Experience

In a letter from an 83 year old woman she said: I was going through the grave yard in my car and a spaceship came down over me, near enough that had I been in a tree I could have touched it. There were no words, nothing but a sensation that was too glorious to mention. I was hypnotized by the heavenly music and the mind impressions of a love I had never felt in all my 83 years. I jumped out of my car, raised my arms and yelled "Hallelujah!" Tears were streaming down my face. I know this may not make much sense to you, but I learned volumes through that incident.

Guidelines for Space Ships Sightings

Following are some guidelines as to how best to handle the situation of UFO's being ridiculed in your present day society:

The best course of action is neither to deny them nor go overboard in insisting that you can make contact. Only the very spiritually advanced can really be in contact with them at any rate. Others may occasionally see them and this is due to misjudgment on the part of those in the ships. They will not normally wish to be seen and therefore can choose not to be, but are occasionally taken by surprise and in some rare instances those in the ships use poor judgment as to becoming visible.

You see we have this choice but whether or not we are visible, rest assured we are here. Those of higher evolutionary standing will not be seen as this has no meaning to them. They have no wish for personal admiration or glorification. They remain inner-spacemen only and are only wishing to help the spiritual understanding of those on the earth plane.

Those doing abductions are from lower evolutionary status. They are not from your solar system and are not part of the designed help to be given to planet earth. They are doing their abductions to further their own understanding and cannot help humans in their spiritual evolvement. One must learn to discriminate between the good guys and the bad guys. If one works hard enough to reach higher level consciousness he will be in touch with the inner space men who can warn him about the outer space men. Those from within your solar system are those who are to guide you into a higher spiritual understanding. They most always will appear only through the inner eye vision. Those from the outer realms of the galaxy are not here to help humans grow spiritually. They are trying to update their own understanding of the universe. Which category does your space flights fall into? Master

As stated the outer spacemen are those on a lower evolutionary rung from another solar system. They have not the ability nor the desire to further spiritual growth and understanding on your earth plane. They basically are self-serving. They like to titillate and tease and play games. They are the ones responsible for cattle mutilations for the purposes of furthering their own understanding of life on planet earth.

229

They are the ones who abduct members of your different races and have taken them back to their home planets. A lot of your disappearing people have been abducted this way. Most who think they were taken up in ships and have lost several hours of earth time were taken usually by "inner-space men." In other words, these people went into a forward moving time escape hatch brought about by their own need, the desperate need of their soul for a true spiritual experience of which the personality knows nothing. This forward progression in time has to take place for any to see or communicate with the inner spacemen which are your guides, (or the hierarchy or guardian angels, or whatever you choose to call them).

It has not always been thus. In the early days of colonization of earth we inner spacemen did choose to materialize and it was much easier then due to the clear, unadulterated atmosphere around your planet. The more heavily polluted earth becomes the harder for us to materialize. It is not as hard for those outside your solar system as they do not have as high a vibration rate as do we.

It will seem like a desecration to some to have us say this but true spirituality on earth is directly tied to pollution of earth. Those groups working for clean atmospheric conditions are doing more for humanity than any church or any group of UFO watchers.

UFO watchers can continue for years chasing here and there and trying to make contact exoterically. This will not, cannot, happen until they can make contact esoterically unless it is of a lower quality of spaceship from outside your solar system. We are waiting for them to contact us esoterically. When enough can accomplish this, then we will choose to land and contact them.

Education is the only way to handle the fact of the existence of space ships, but certainly not situations that set up the opportunity for ridicule. Education of spaceships being with earth from the beginning is the best way to start. As we said before, there is more truth in most Greek mythology and even other stories and myths than there is in your Bible and this certainly must be the starting point.

True spirituality cannot be prevalent on earth until we are understood. Humanity must begin to tie in the fact of space ships and space flights to the Bible tales and they will all become so obvious. Take every saying that has been repeated for the last 2000 years and interpret it from the angle of a universal citizen. All that is needed is common sense. We are here to help humanity stay in balance, but not into phenomena. We are not "figments of your imagination," but we are also not "clowns in a circus act." We are the Sons and Daughters of God, your elder Brothers and Sisters.

The Musical Universe (Outside Our Solar System)

There are times when the need for higher information allows the channel to connect with higher beings. This was the case recently when the following came through.

We are the Musical Universe. We are not in a space ship as you, Norma, just wondered. We are free floating, but we do not have the need for that type of form. We can be anywhere in any universe that we wish. We are the original subatomic particles that came from the first bits of condensation in the universe. We are, if you will, the original Adam and Eve to relate it to stories fostered unintelligently on your earth plane. This will all change soon. There will be a new book of facts that you will bring into being, that will not be able to be denied by any.

The musical universe is full of all sorts of ideas, so numerous and so easy to apply that we are amazed that more use is not being made of them. It is, we suppose, because there has not been contact with us before now, but this is changed. We deem it highly advisable that this channel be used primarily for contact with this musical universe. We believe her capabilities should be made available to many different organizations for questions to be fed into the musical universe. This alone could speed up evolutionary progress for both the planet and the human by hundreds of years, just by this channel's output during the remainder of her life. As it is now, this rare, beautiful, meaningful, useful talent is stagnating. We are impressing her to offer these services to scientific foundations worldwide. There is so much available that it is frustrating to not be able to see it in use on the earth plane. You will never know how frustrating because you cannot be in the position to know. The musical universe is closed to those of evolutionary progression. All those on evolutionary worlds will not be able to progress to this universe. It is made up of those who chose to not ever incarnate on an evolutionary planet. We have lived our whole beingness as a musical vibration and cannot ever take on a physical body. But we can cultivate contact with one on your plane and have been doing so for the past five incarnations of this channel. We have groomed her and taught her and provided for her and we would like to be able to see the fruits of our labor over the past several centuries.

As musical vibrations, we were from the first universe, the very first puff of evolution after the original manifestation in sound took place. We are the remnants of the half of the atom that remained positive energy as manifestation of sound. The evolutionary worlds are remnants of the half of the atom that manifested in the color kingdom. The vibrations of the colors are not as intense as those of sound. The creator of the manifestation of color, the half of the atom that spawned the evolutionary worlds was absorbed in the explosion and those from the world of color come under the guidance and love and protection of the half of the atom that remained and is generating the life force, the hydrogen atom. Therefore, you have the same guidance and love and protection as we do, but are from the other half of the atom, the negative half of the atom. This is the main difference between the evolutionary worlds and the spiritual worlds. You have been given before that you will never progress to a spiritual world when you are from an evolutionary world, but will have the opportunity to associate and learn and study with us and exchange information back and forth.

As far as our life in the musical universe we are "stationed" here as the first stop in our journey when we come from the One Creator as a brand new subatomic particle. This is where the strongest vibrations are. These vibrations were stepped down as each universe developed. As we move from here on to the next in our journey we mellow our tone out. As it is now we are very strong, sharp and piercing tones. We need to have an outlet for our energy and this is the frustration that leads us to evolve through the universe, the same as it is your will to do so because of frustration. We will eventually end up in the same place but will still be separated by degree of vibration. There is no way anyone from the evolutionary worlds can ever become one of us. It is against universal law.

Our life is a dance of the most glorious kind. We have groups of mates that we harmonize with at different times in our journey, but they will always be those in perfect harmony with the intent of our evolvement. For instance, one of us with the tone of F would not ever mate up with one on the tone of F#. There is no harmony there. There would never be an attraction to begin with. The work we do covers the whole universe as far as tending to the vibratory rates of all the solidified bodies. This is our task, keeping the universe in perfect tune harmonically. This is why we have been training this channel, to help raise your planet's vibratory field. Not only this channel, but others are helping raise it, but this channel in particular can do much more in the actual field of vibrations than the others because of her contact with us. We feel we must close this off for now because our energy is very strong and the channel should not be allowed to remain open as long. Thank you very much for this opportunity to express. We await the next becoming. Good day.

Made in the USA
Las Vegas, NV
27 April 2022

48060826R00134